Communications
for
progress

First published 1990 by

Catholic Institute for International Relations (CIIR),
22 Coleman Fields, London N1 7AF, UK

and:

Antenna/Interdoc, PO Box 1513, 6501 BM Nijmegen, Netherlands

Environment & Development Resource Centre (EDRC),
Blvd. Louis Schmidtlaan 26, 1040 Brussels, Belgium

British Library Cataloguing in Publications Data
    Lane, Graham
    Communications for Progress: a guide to international e-mail
    1. Electronic mail systems
    I. Title
    384.34
    ISBN 1-85287-069-9

Cover and text design by Rich Cowley
Text illustrations by David Styan
Typeset and printed in England by the Russell Press Ltd,
Bertrand Russell House, Gamble Street, Nottingham NG7 4ET

Communications
for
progress

*A guide to international
e-mail*

Graham Lane

   EDRC INTERDOC

To Chris, Mischa and Kai

Contents

PART ONE: GENERAL

1: Telecommunications: an overview

2: E-mail

3: Case studies

PART TWO: TECHNICAL

4: Hardware and software

Diagrams

Acknowledgements

Staff from the organisations that are used as case studies in Chapter Three took time to complete a questionnaire and answer many additional questions. Several of the entries are based closely on their original replies.

Special thanks are due to the following people: Heinz Hunke and his colleagues at IDOC, Tim Jackson, Sheila O'Sullivan (AHRTAG), Paul Osborn (Satis), Sister Mary Pignone (Sisters of Notre Dame), Michael Polman (Antenna) and Steve Walker (Poptel/GeoNet). All of them read drafts of the book and made many valuable comments.

Comments or correspondence concerning this book are welcome and may be addressed to Graham Lane, c/o CIIR (contact details on page 141).

IF ALL ELSE FAILS — READ THE INSTRUCTIONS

Foreword

Writing on technical matters for a non-technical audience is very difficult, especially if this audience is traditionally not always in favour of modern technologies. Yet **Communications for Progress** combines a comprehensive introduction to the world of electronic networking with an appetising invitation for non-governmental organisations (NGOs) to join the global 'on-line' community. I appreciate Graham Lane's work even more knowing that he started as most users, learning by 'trial and error'. But he went much further and shared his experiences with others by writing this book. Because he wrote it from the user perspective, it became not a dull techno-speak book but an invaluable guide to a new field of computer communications for NGOs that will be welcomed all over the world.

This is the first book to introduce and explain the new telecommunication technologies that are the vehicles of global electronic networking between thousands of NGOs. NGO e-mail users have been crying out for a guide such as this. Aware of their need, I myself had planned to produce a book along the lines of **Communications for Progress** — Graham Lane's publication has meant that I can start work on a technical companion volume for more advanced NGO facilitators. This will be published by Antenna towards the end of 1990.

On the nature of NGO networks

Most NGOs trade in information for social change. Some focus on collecting information, some on analysing it and others on its dissemination. NGOs have become independent intelligence centres specialising either in a region or on a specific topic. They provide a uniquely wide-ranging source of information from a variety of communities, counterbalancing that traditionally supplied by governments and businesses. If access to information can change both attitudes and policies, then the NGO perspective can assist social change.

When NGOs share information and resources their effectiveness improves. Costs are minimal, as information stored in computers can be copied at little expense and as often as one desires. Exchanging information is therefore a 'profitable' investment.

Cutting out the 'dead wood'

Networking fits the nature of NGOs like a glove. It supports the informal non-hierarchical exchange of information, it helps lateral communication and decentralised cooperation, and it cuts out unnecessary forms of bureaucratic 'dead wood'. NGOs can benefit from networking much more than organisations such as governments and corporations that depend on hierarchical and centralised control. Yet there can be no networking without communication. The introduction of cheap and immediate international communication based on linking microcomputers with the global datacommunication networks has therefore greatly encouraged the development of NGO networks.

Electronic 'post offices' (or mailbox hosts) have become platforms for international information exchange and interdisciplinary cooperation. These mailbox host systems provide electronic mail, telex and telefax services at non-commercial rates, enabling almost any NGO on this globe to participate in the exchange of information, provided that it has access to a microcomputer and a telephone line. Hundreds of electronic bulletins covering numerous issues are available free on most e-mail systems, encouraging international discussions. These bulletin boards function as on-going conferences and informal NGO news services, often more detailed and up-to-date than traditional news services. They enable NGOs to send out alerts or to seek support for their work 24 hours a day. The endangerment, arrests or murders of people in Chernobyl, Malaysia, China and Colombia were all known to the international on-line NGO community within hours of these violations occurring.

The 'critical mass'

Every day new NGOs join one of the dozens of NGO mailbox systems and networks. The networks have swelled to a 'critical mass' of members so eager to join that they have become part of an irreversible and uncontrollable process, producing an unimaginable flood of information. Already just one of the mailbox host systems, Poptel/GeoNet, with a few hundred NGO members of whom many are based in the South, makes possible the exchange of more than 200 Megabytes of data per month — a total of 50,000 pages. A new global community is forming, larger than any other international organisation, a community constantly expanding and reproducing itself.

The new electronic communication networks have brought about more than one revolution in the NGO world. In terms of communications, the smallest NGO in the South can now be on an equal footing with other NGOs, the media, funding agencies, large corporations, governments or the United Nations. Functioning more and more as well-informed platforms and interest groups, NGOs can now overcome the rivalry amongst them that marked the early 1980s. Electronic networking has also facilitated the democratisation of high technology, regarded in the early 1980s as strictly for government or corporate use. 'Hacking' this technology has given grassroots organisations access to virtually all sources of information. It has enabled NGOs to monitor the inevitable internationalisation of their economies and decision-making. Gradually the international NGO community is creating its own global ideologies, responding to the activities of intergovernmental institutions and transnational corporations in the fields of the environment, employment, food, health and education. There are now NGO networks providing information on all of these issues and more: deforestation, foreign debt, labour, human rights and AIDS. Electronic networking is enabling the grassroots to participate in the solving of global problems and, in the process, the cultural and ideological divides between North and South, East and West, are slowly being bridged.

Some negative aspects

No one can escape from the social, political and cultural effects of adopting modern technology. Electronic networking supports new forms of cooperation that strengthen NGO networks, but it also demands technical language and concepts that alienate other forms of communication. In order to reduce the costs, language becomes more and more compact, efficient and 'bloodless'. Symbols replace emotional statements and the elaboration of any issue, no matter how important, is avoided to save money and time. Printing on paper becomes obsolete, so computer illiterates tend to be excluded from discussions on vital issues in the NGO communities and networks. Having no mailbox becomes as insulating as having no postal address or telephone. A divide is being created within and between some NGOs where networking was once seen as bringing people together. Most NGOs, however, argue that this new technology assists their work so much that these negative aspects should be overlooked.

Another danger for NGOs participating in international networks is that of maintaining contact with their constituencies: the grassroots organisations. Daily link-ups with electronic post offices tend to demand increasing amounts of attention and time — the more news you send out the more messages you receive. Traditional channels of communication are being neglected in favour of fast and immediate global 'on-line' networking. This can affect not only the focus of those people working with 'on-line' communications, but also the policies of NGOs. Their work with grassroots organisations may suffer seriously as a result.

Traditional relationships between partner organisations are changing in many respects. Funding agencies are being overwhelmed by requests from NGOs and are finding it difficult to cope with so much new information and its internal distribution. Their allocation of funds benefits those NGOs that are 'on-line', as the process of accepting projects for funding can now be dealt with in days or weeks rather than months. Funding agencies must devise a policy on working with the growing number of NGO networks: on the one hand they must invest their funds more efficiently, but on the other hand they must meet the challenge of much larger interest groups.

In some cases the implementation of electronic networking seems to have created very 'pale and male' dominated networks, be it in the North or the South. There is a distinct lack of

xiv

participation by women and Third World indigenous communities. Modern technology appears to attract more northern, white and male users than anyone else. Furthermore, the 'sex appeal' of fashionable new technologies attracts more users than do the political possibilities of networking.

There is a real need for news received via electronic mail to be shared and for the skills required to access electronic networks to be passed on within NGOs. This is often overlooked. To enter the world of electronic mail is normally to be swept up in a whirlwind of on-line requests, files and messages. The excitement of belonging to a 'global community' overshadows the negative aspects. You hardly notice or care that your front door is shut most of the time and that your window on the outside world has become less important than the computer screen. There you have a direct link with the open sky, via satellites suspended 30,000 km above the earth, with thousands of other NGOs all around the world: truly a very attractive, but also a distracting perspective.

Facing the future
As the 21st century approaches, our global society is rapidly changing. We are witnesses to an escalation of international economic structures, a press and broadcasting media able to offer instant access to the rest of the world, mass human migration, mass tourism ... A global culture is emerging, slowly but surely. The world is getting smaller but the gap between North and South continues to grow. The poor remain poor, the 'have-nots' remain 'have-nots'.

The introduction of e-mail offers a tantalising new internationalist and interdisciplinary tool for all those who work for social change. These telecommunication technologies have opened up new means of cooperating and of exchanging information on a global scale at an affordable price. Electronic networking will inevitably change the nature and culture of NGOs, giving us a new challenge: how best to effect information exchange in order to achieve social change.

Michael Polman, ANTENNA, June 1990

Introduction

Together with fax and telex, computer communications play an important role in the day to day work of an ever increasing number of organisations. Computer communication can take various forms. One form involves the direct link up of two machines, possibly across the telephone network. Once the connection is established, data is transferred back and forth between the two parties. Electronic mail — or e-mail — is another form of computer communication. E-mail users may swap text messages, computer files or programs — but they do it via a large, central computer. It is essentially a 'pigeon hole' system. Any computer user who is a member of the e-mail system can call up the central computer via the telephone network and leave messages in the 'mailboxes' of other subscribers. At a later point the recipients will call the central host computer and collect their unread mail.

E-mail is different from the direct transfer of data between two parties. It can, in certain circumstances, have advantages in terms of compatibility and cost — particularly on international calls. E-mail is generally most relevant as a public system for exchanging information. Direct computer links, on the other hand, may be more appropriate in special situations when the two parties are known to one another.

It will not be particularly expensive or disruptive for an organisation which is already using microcomputers to adopt e-mail as a supplement to its existing channels of communication. It is being adopted by more and more organisations in the non-commercial sector.

Every day non-governmental organisations (NGOs), charities, campaigning groups, resource centres and similar bodies exchange information using e-mail. The exchange of information may be within one country or it may be international. E-mail is a truly worldwide phenomenon, not simply confined to developed countries; it is used in Managua and Manila as much as Manchester and Melbourne. Organisations working for social progress use e-mail to broadcast press releases, to coordinate joint actions, to circulate appeals and so forth. On a 'one to one' basis it is a cheap and efficient method for national or international correspondence. E-mail is also a powerful tool in research work. With a computer and modem a researcher can efficiently and cheaply publicise requests for information, correspond with contacts around the world, and search databases for relevant material.

The use of e-mail is well established in environmental and peace groups and organisations dealing with the rights of indigenous peoples. The US-based PeaceNet is a pioneering example of a non-profit e-mail system. There are now several similar systems around the world, including GreenNet in Britain. Calendars of events, information on forthcoming activities and on-going discussion on a vast array of relevant topics are all features of these systems.

Development agencies and charities are now rapidly adopting e-mail. Such organisations often have overseas offices in developing countries. They are particularly attracted to e-mail by the prospect of improved internal communications and potential financial savings. In addition, many of them have some form of research or public education department. On top of internal administrative uses, e-mail can be used by these organisations for information exchange and networking.

Computer communications also play an important role in the work of media groups. Besides using computer communication for the speedy transfer of information, several respected organisations also use e-mail to publish 'on-line magazines', available to all e-mail users. Such bulletins are not restricted to developed countries. The best ones are a valuable source of on-the-spot reports and analyses.

Trade unions are, with some exceptions, not currently large users of e-mail. There is, however, every reason to expect that this situation could change. A number of large unions are currently evaluating e-mail, which appears to have a number of benefits to offer in relation to the work and structure of unions. The potential union network is huge.

In addition to improved communications, experienced e-mail users are beginning to discover the potential for information retrieval from 'on-line' database services. These databases are huge collections of information which can be dialled up from a computer and searched for relevant material. Searching is by combinations of 'key' words or phrases (such as 'Chile' and 'election'). The result will be a list of references or extracts of relevant text. Such databases can either be contacted by a direct call or via e-mail systems. At present most of them are either commercial in orientation or they are built up of material taken from newspapers and magazines. They can be an extremely useful source of information on companies, economic or political trends, current events and so forth. The main drawback is that they are expensive.

The present growth in computer communications in the non-commercial sector is beginning to stimulate the development of a new class of databases. The primary aim of these databases is to make information widely available to concerned organisations. The charges will generally be a fraction of current commercial rates. An example is a database of all the judgments of the European Court of Human Rights in Strasbourg, which it is planned to make available on-line to national human rights organisations working through the Human Rights Documentation Centre of the Court. Cheap and easy access to such information is potentially of great benefit to national organisations working on refugee and asylum cases.

There are a number of similar projects currently under development. The coming period will witness the creation of major databases carrying information from NGOs worldwide. There are many possibilities both for organisations wishing to make information available and for organisations seeking information. In this respect, e-mail is simply a stepping stone on the route to a far wider electronic interchange of information between non-commercial organisation.

There is every indication that a 'community' of non-commercial e-mail users is developing. The work of many non-commercial organisations is directed quite consciously

xviii

towards making resources available, cooperating with similar groups and broadcasting relevant information. Any group involved in educational work is basically outward-looking. E-mail is a powerful tool in this kind of work. The strengths of e-mail are ideally suited to the development of partner networking and the open exchange of information.

The take-up of computer communications in the business and commercial sector has, by contrast, been patchy. On the strong side are large multinational companies that have, without exception, installed huge and highly sophisticated computer systems. The work of such organisations would collapse without the constant transfer of computer data. E-mail is simply a small — but important — element in the functioning of these systems. It is, for example, useful for interconnecting the divisions of a company located in different time zones and on different continents. The important point to note, however, is that the whole operation is private. It is run on computers and communications lines owned by a given company. In this respect such systems are different from the public e-mail systems used by NGOs. On a different level, access to financial information and political analyses from commercial databases is an essential part of the activity of many companies and media organisations. At the other end of the scale, however, many smaller companies have adopted fax rather than e-mail. These organisations are primarily concerned with efficient 'point to point' communications. The boom in fax in the West has confounded the original predictions of many pundits concerning the projected uptake of e-mail.

It is dangerous to draw too sharp a distinction between the commercial world and the non-commercial world. The object of the preceding discussion has been simply to highlight the fact that e-mail can have quite specific advantages to offer for the non-commercial sector. As an international community, the non-commercial sector is succeeding in creating a specific identity based on common outlook, aims and requirements. This can only help to encourage cooperation and the pooling of scarce resources nationally and worldwide.

The adoption of information technology by many small and medium-sized organisations is taking place in series of waves. The first is the installation of computers for tasks such as word processing, accounting and information storage. Such development is a direct result of the appearance of cheap but powerful computers — the microcomputer 'revolution' of the early 1980s. The second is the further exploitation of microcomputer power to improve and increase communication between like-minded organisations. This happens particularly through the development of appropriate e-mail systems and partner networks. The third wave that will break over us in the coming years is the creation of database systems aimed at the needs of non-commercial organisations. We will then witness the full potential of information technology harnessed in the cause of progress and social justice.

This book deals primarily with the second wave: e-mail and computer communications. However, in order to understand the significance of e-mail we can afford to neglect neither our background nor our aims.

This book is quite consciously written from the perspective of someone working in a non-governmental organisation (NGO). This necessitates a short warning for potential British readers since British books on e-mail almost invariably have an extensive section about the largest British e-mail system, Telecom Gold. This book doesn't. The reason for this is simple. Telecom Gold (part of the Dialcom network) is not particularly popular amongst the kind of organisations that are the focus of this book. Instead these organisations tend to use the GeoMail system or one of the systems grouped together under the umbrella of the Association for Progressive Communications (APC). These systems offer special facilities for non-commercial organisations and they are a good deal cheaper than Telecom Gold.

As far as possible this book is not tied to any particular e-mail system or software package. Most of the information will therefore be of relevance to users of Telecom Gold, GeoMail, APC or any other e-mail system. Certainly the technical information will be of more or less universal relevance. In this sense, the book should be useful for anyone in a small or medium-sized organisation, be it in the commercial or non-commercial world.

Every effort has been made to ensure that all the material will be accessible to a reader who has no prior knowledge of e-mail or data communications. It is, however, assumed that readers will at some stage have laid their hands on a microcomputer, most probably for word processing. No effort is made to explain general computer terms such as 'disc' or 'software'. Explanations are, however, given for all jargon terms — such as 'modem' or 'comms software' — that relate specifically to e-mail. There is also a glossary of technical terms at the end of the text. For potential new users of e-mail, there are appendices giving a step by step guide to getting on-line, and some useful contact addresses.

PART ONE
GENERAL

PART ONE: GENERAL

Chapters 1-3

Part One of this guide gives a general introduction to the field of telecommunications and e-mail. Chapter 1 examines telex, fax and computer communication including e-mail. Chapter 2 takes a more detailed look at e-mail, highlighting its strengths and examining the concept of 'networking'. The final chapter in Part One contains a series of short case studies of non-commercial organisations which are using e-mail.

Telecommunications: an overview

1

The aim of this chapter is to put e-mail in perspective by comparing it with other forms of telecommunication. Telecommunication refers to the whole field of the transmission of information over the telephone system or similar public and private networks. There are four forms of telecommunication that may be encountered in the non-commercial sector: telex, fax, direct computer to computer communications, and computer based e-mail systems.

This chapter does not aim to provide any hard and fast rules about when it is 'best' to use any particular form of communication. It is impossible to be so specific. In real life each situation will be different and will demand its own particular solution. Communication by post or telephone will be entirely adequate in certain circumstances. It is worth bearing in mind, however, that the postal service is slow and very unreliable in some developing countries. It may not be a viable method for regular communication.

Small organisations and individuals may be restricted by lack of resources to only one method of communication. In this situation e-mail may be an attractive option. Larger organisations, on the other hand, will be seeking to integrate different technologies so that they complement one another in an overall plan for communications.

E-mail offers certain specific advantages which can be of tremendous benefit in particular types of work. It is, however, a mistake to imagine that e-mail is some kind of magic formula which is set to replace other methods of communication. It is not.

Telex

Telex is an acronym for 'teleprinter exchange'. In the USA the telex system is run by various private networks. In other parts of the world the telex system is often run by the state. The national telex networks around the world are inter-linked in an international system.

Telex grew out of telegraphy. The original telegraph system was based on trained operators sending messages in Morse code between fixed telegraph offices. Telex introduced two major enhancements to this system. Firstly, the telegraph or Morse key was replaced by the teleprinter. A teleprinter consists of a keyboard and a printer. This allowed any trained typist to send messages. Secondly, teleprinters were installed on the premises of businesses. It was no longer necessary to go to the telegraph office to send and receive messages. The telex system is made up of teleprinters connected across a telegraph-style network. Every teleprinter — or telex terminal — has a unique identification number like a telephone number. The telex network is, however, different from the telephone network. The two systems use different technologies to transmit messages. There are a number of variants on the original telex network. Some of the modern variations transmit messages across the telephone network rather than the telex network.

The original telex system provided a viable means of long-distance text transmission far in advance of other available methods. It was widely adopted by business and came to play a particularly important role in the work of news agencies and the press. Today telex has partly been superseded by other methods of communication. Nonetheless, it is a well-established system and still offers benefits in certain areas.

Description

It is tricky attempting to describe a telex terminal. This is because a wide variety of terminals — ranging from the absolutely ancient to the absolutely modern — are in daily use around the world.

The most rudimentary machines consist of a keyboard and a printer. Sending a message on such a machine simply involves obtaining a connection and then typing the text. As each character is keyed in it is sent straight down the telex line — the typist cannot afford to make any mistakes. Such machines are now rare. An early enhancement was the introduction of punched-hole paper tape. This allowed messages to be prepared on paper tape before transmission. The next development in the evolution of the telex terminal was the addition of memory and a display. As with paper tape systems, terminals with memory allow messages to be prepared 'off-line'. This means that the text is keyed in, edited and saved in memory before it is sent. Such terminals will also have a display that allows the user to review the text of messages stored in memory. The display might only show a few lines at a time. Such terminals will frequently offer automatic re-dial facilities. This is a useful feature since telex terminals are often engaged at the first call attempt.

The most modern telex terminals have a full screen display like the screen of a personal computer, displaying 24 lines of text at a time. Modern terminals may also be equipped with disc drives. These allow an archive of incoming and outgoing messages to be stored on to disc. Only a limited number of messages can be stored in the telex memory before it becomes full. Disc storage, by contrast, offers unlimited archiving capacity. It is also possible to link a microcomputer directly to a modern telex terminal. In this way a computer-based word processing package can be used to prepare text before transferring it to the telex terminal for transmission.

One further option is actually to use a microcomputer as a telex terminal. This is done by adding an external 'telex box' or fitting an internal 'telex card' to the micro. In Britain a telex box or telex card costs a little over half the price of a proper telex terminal. This may represent a saving in cases of light telex usage. For heavier usage, however, the savings involved will be offset by the fact that the microcomputer will be in use for substantial periods when sending and reading telexes.

Advantages

The advantages of telex in relation to fax or e-mail are confined to certain specific areas. Firstly, telex is widely used in developing countries. This is partly because it is a more long-established means of communication and developing countries have had time to develop a telex network. It will remain important in countries that cannot afford the rapid development necessary to keep pace with more modern communications technology. This means that telex will continue to be useful in the field of news and media.

Secondly, telex transmissions are very robust. Whereas fax transmissions may suffer badly from interference due to 'line noise', a telex transmission will generally either go through correctly or, in rare cases, abort. This helps to explain the popularity of telex in developing countries where the quality of the phone lines (used for fax and e-mail) may be poor.

Finally, telex messages are widely accepted as having some form of legal status. A telex message — placing an order, for example — is commonly accepted as a legally binding contract. The same is not currently true of fax or e-mail messages.

Disadvantages

The chief drawback of telex is cost. In most parts of the world a telex terminal will cost more than a cheap hard disc microcomputer. There is a heavy charge for the installation of a new telex line and rental charges for the line are higher than equivalent telephone charges. In addition, a telex transmission is slow in comparison to fax or e-mail, which serves to further increase running costs. Unlike most telephone systems, there is no cheap rate for telex calls.

The installation of a new telex terminal is unlikely to be an attractive option unless telex offers some particular benefit over other forms of communication. The continued viability of the telex network rests mainly on the existing base of established telex users. Yet telex has lost its position as the principal means of long-distance text transmission. In several European countries the total number of telex connections is now beginning to fall. However, the decline is gradual. There is a trend, for the medium term at least, towards the integration of telex as one element in a broader range of telecommunications options.

Cheaper options for using telex

As mentioned above, a microcomputer can double as a telex terminal if fitted with a telex box or card. This is cheaper than a proper telex terminal. There is, however, no reduction in the costs of installing and renting a telex line and there is no reduction in running costs.

Organisations which only use telex occasionally may opt to use a 'telex bureau'. This is a form of outside office, operated by a third party which sends and receives telex messages. The user simply sends the message through to the bureau, possibly by phone, and it is sent on as a telex. In a similar manner, notification is sent by phone and post when an incoming telex is received. Most e-mail systems offer the possibility of sending and receiving telex, like a telex bureau. There is more on this in the last section of this chapter.

Fax

Fax is an abbreviation of the term facsimile. Fax transmission is used to send a copy of a document over a telephone line. The source document could, for example, be printed material, a photograph, or a handwritten message and could include diagrams or drawings.

A fax machine consists of a scanner, a modem and a printer. The source document is 'scanned' as it is fed into the sending machine. Successive small rectangles of the document — known as 'pixels' — are examined to determine whether they are black or white. The resulting information is stored in binary form — that is to say as a series of 1s or 0s representing black and white. This is know as 'digitisation' of the image. A sheet of A4 will be divided into more than three million pixels during scanning by an ordinary business fax machine. More sophisticated machines use even smaller pixels and may be able to detect a series of grey tones. The digitised information is transmitted over a telephone line and printed out by the distant machine in a process which is the reverse of the scanning procedure.

High quality fax has long been used for specialist purposes, such as the transmission of photographs by news agencies. In recent years, however, there has been a tremendous boom in the use of fax by businesses.

Current business fax machines are known as class 3 machines. The group or class in question is a CCITT standard. CCITT is a highly influential body, linked to the United Nations, which develops standards for telecommunications. All class 3 fax machines are mutually compatible regardless of manufacturer.

They are sometimes — but not always — capable of communicating with older class 2 machines. An even more advanced standard for group 4 fax has also been defined but it will be some years before these machines become widespread. There are two major developments in the current generation of fax machines which in part account for their rapid growth in popularity. Firstly, they are small in comparison to older cabinet-sized machines. A modern fax machine will fit comfortably on a desk top. There are portable fax machines on the market. It is also possible to fit an expansion card inside a microcomputer which will allow it to send and receive fax. The second improvement is a great increase in transmission speeds. A group 3 machine can send a normal typewritten A4 page in around 30 seconds — about six times faster than a group 2 machine. The actual transmission time depends on the amount and density of text. Documents with a lot of blank space go quickly while high density source documents, such as photos, are slow.

Group 3 machines are normally equipped with printers that use a technique known as thermal printing. Such printers give reasonable quality output but need special heat sensitive paper. The paper is expensive. In certain circumstances the printout may fade with time. In due course, thermal printing techniques in fax may be superseded by laser printing. This produces a higher quality output and allows the use of ordinary paper.

The cost of a fax transmission is the same as the cost of an equivalent voice telephone call. The fax machine monitors the quality of the line during transmission. If it registers interference it will print a warning that errors may have occurred. Otherwise most machines will confirm successful transmission and give the duration of the call.

Fax machines
There is a wide variety of fax machines even within the field of standard class 3 business models. The range includes portable fax, mid-range models and sophisticated machines with memory.

Standard mid-range office fax offer a number of features that enhance the operation of the machine. A sheet feeder, for example, will allow anything up to 50 sheets to be stacked ready for automatic transmission. A guillotine will cut messages into A4 sheets as they are printed. Short code dialling is another common feature that allows frequently used fax telephone numbers to be stored under one or two-key codes for easy dialling. Automatic re-dial is a useful facility found on most machines. If a number is engaged, the fax will automatically re-try a certain number of times at pre-determined intervals. Portable fax, on the other hand, sacrifice many of these features in pursuit of compactness and lightness. Most can only feed one sheet at a time and are not equipped with a guillotine.

Top range fax models are provided with memory, like the memory of a computer. Fax memory is particularly valuable for sending a document to multiple destinations. In order to send a document to 30 destinations using a non-memory machine it is necessary to feed the original through the machine 30 times. The document is re-scanned for each transmission. Using a memory fax, by contrast, it is only necessary to feed the original through the machine once. The 'image' of the document is stored in the memory and can be re-sent. A memory fax, however, may cost around twice the price of a machine without memory.

PC-fax

A recent development is to equip a microcomputer to function as a fax terminal. This is done by installing a 'fax card' inside the computer. A PC-fax card carries all the necessary fax circuitry and is normally easy to fit. It is a good deal cheaper than a standard fax machine because it uses the computer's printer and sends messages direct from the computer memory. It dispenses with the need for separate scanning and printing equipment. A fax card can use the memory of the computer to offer all the advantages of a top-range memory fax machine.

There are certain drawbacks to PC-fax cards. The computer user will, for example, only be able to send plain text messages or graphics produced in a limited number of graphics software packages. It is possible to merge graphics and text files so that an organisation logo or heading can be inserted at the top of a letter. To transmit more complex graphics, however, requires investing in a separate, expensive scanner to attach to the computer. Furthermore, the actual conversion of a computer text

9

file into a form suitable for fax transmission is slow except on powerful computers. In addition, it may take a long time to print out a fax transmission that contains graphics.

The main disadvantage of PC-fax cards, however, is that incoming text messages are received by the computer as a graphic image rather than as a text file. The fax can be printed out and — possibly — accessed in a graphics software package but the message is still an 'image'. It cannot, for example, be directly edited in a word processing package. Optical Character Recognition (OCR) software may attempt to 'read' an image and convert individual letters into the form of a normal computer text file but such techniques are new and unreliable. They may develop in the future.

Advantages

Ease of use: One sure reason for the current boom in business fax is that fax machines are so easy to use. Some people still find microcomputers quite intimidating. A fax machine, on the other hand, may be even easier to operate than an advanced office photo-copying machine. There is no expense or delay resulting from the need for staff training on fax.

Graphics: Another big plus is that fax can transmit graphics such as drawings, diagrams, photos, handwritten messages etc. As an example, it is possible to send copies of newspaper clippings by fax. This has great potential for some forms of international information exchange.

Non-Latin scripts: Linked to the ability to send graphics is the possibility of quickly and simply transmitting messages in non-Latin scripts. Computer communications, by contrast, are often heavily geared towards the English alphabet. It is awkward to send e-mail messages in other scripts. For this reason fax is particularly well-established in Japan.

Disadvantages

Cost: A potential disadvantage of fax is the capital cost of a new fax machine — although, in Britain at least, prices are still dropping. For regular office use a telephone line reserved solely for fax is also needed. The installation of a new line is expensive and will involve a long wait in some countries. In cases of light usage only, it may be possible for a fax machine and a telephone to share a line.

The running cost of fax is related to the telephone charges incurred and paper usage. The cost of the special thermal paper rolls — required by most fax machines — is not negligible. There is no reduction in cost for sending multiple copies of a document. Even though a memory fax only scans a document once there is still a charge for each transmission. The cost of a single document sent to 30 destinations will be the sum of the 30 individual calls. It is clearly not an ideal method of circulating a press release, for example. Multiple transmission of a single source document is much cheaper when using e-mail, as explained below.

Re-typing: It may be necessary to re-type edited fax messages for re-transmission. In certain situations this can be a major headache. It would, for example, be an impractical method for groups to circulate drafts of a joint report.

Line noise: Line noise is interference on a telephone line that may corrupt a transmission. A bad line could easily make parts of a fax quite unreadable. E-mail can overcome this problem by 'error correction' techniques. These provide for the re-transmission of a corrupted sections until all have been received error free. The current generation of fax machines, however, do not provide any standard form of error correction. An international agreement for fax error correction does exist but it will be some time before this comes into widespread usage.

For the present, line noise can be a serious problem on fax transmissions to developing countries. Not only is it frustrating and time consuming to re-send a document several times but it is also very expensive. If it takes six attempts to send a fax without corruption then the telephone charge will be for six calls — even if these are expensive international calls.

PART ONE: GENERAL

Direct computer-to-computer links

This method of communication quite simply involves the direct transfer of information from one computer to another. It is different from e-mail, which is described in the next section. The two computers could be standing next to one another linked by a cable or they could be on opposite sides of the world linked by a telephone line. If the connection is through a telephone line, then each computer will need to be fitted with a small device called a modem. Whatever kind of link is used, both computers will also need to use a software program for communications. Such programs regulate the flow of data into and out of the computer. There is more on modems and communications software in Chapter 4.

Direct computer to computer communication requires quite a high level of coordination between the two parties. Various technical and procedural aspects of the transfer must be agreed beforehand. For this reason direct computer links are only practical between users who are known to one another. This could be between different offices of the same organisation or between a small circle of organisations that have agreed on a pre-arranged system. For example, one user — the answering end — might prepare a number of files ready for transmission. At a given time the computer and modem are made ready to answer an incoming call. With some (but not all) communications software packages it will still be possible to continue using the computer for other tasks, such as word processing, while waiting for the incoming call. The computer and modem at the answering end cannot, however, be turned off and the modem must be plugged in to the telephone line. At a pre-determined time the 'calling' party dials through to the waiting modem and establishes a direct connection. The designated files can then be transferred from one machine to the other. With the correct preparation it is possible to effect such a transfer even if the 'answering' end is unattended.

A lengthy file transfer can quickly build up high telephone charges. In many instances, therefore, the advantages of a direct computer link-up will have to be weighed against the possibility of simply sending a disc through the post.

Advantages

An advantage of direct computer-to-computer communication is that quite high speeds of data transfer can be achieved. It may also be possible to use sophisticated techniques for the correction of errors due to line noise. Such techniques may not be available on public systems. High speed transmission with error correction requires more expensive modems than those used for ordinary e-mail. There may, however, be situations in which the savings resulting from faster transmission justify the additional costs of the modem.

Direct computer link-ups may also be an option for communication from developing countries that do not have packet switching. Packet switching is a technique that reduces the costs of data transfer relative to normal telephone charges (Chapter 7 gives more details). E-mail may not be feasible in countries that do not have packet switching.

Disadvantages

There must be a high degree of compatibility between the sending and the receiving parties. In the case of high speed transmission, for example, it may even be necessary for the two sides to have identical modems.

Establishing a direct computer link requires a fair degree of technical knowledge — at both ends of the line. It may be possible to establish clear guidelines so that operation of a link-up becomes more or less routine. There is, however, much that can go wrong. If a direct computer link-up is to be used for serious, regular communications then experienced computer users must be available, if needed.

E-mail

The principle of electronic mail — or e-mail — is that computer users swap messages via a large central computer. The large central computer is known as the e-mail host computer. The central host computer is operated by the body which runs the e-mail system. In very large e-mail systems, there may, in fact, be several interlinked host computers rather than just one. From the point of view of the e-mail user, however, the principles of the system are just the same.

Any organisation or individual wishing to use e-mail must first join an e-mail system. In most developed countries there will be a variety of different e-mail systems to choose from. There are a number of systems which specialise in providing services for the non-commercial sector. Similar e-mail systems are now also beginning to appear in some developing countries.

Each member of an e-mail system is assigned a 'mailbox' on the central e-mail host computer. Every mailbox has a unique name or identification code. Passwords are used to prevent unauthorised access to a mailbox. Members of an e-mail system connect up with the central host computer via an ordinary telephone line. A microcomputer is said to be 'on-line' when a direct connection is established with the central host computer. Subscribers swap messages by 'posting' them in each others' mailboxes. In some cases it will also be possible to post messages in the mailboxes of users on other e-mail systems. An e-mail user will not be aware of any new messages until he or she connects up with the central host computer to 'check' their mailbox. Each time a member connects up with the central host computer a message is displayed indicating whether any new mail has been posted in the user's mailbox since the last time they connected up with the system.

E-mail involves a form of computer to computer communications. As such, the microcomputer of an e-mail user must be fitted with a modem and loaded with a software program to control the data transmission. Modems and communications software are discussed in chapter 4. In contrast to direct computer to computer communication, however, the sender and the recipient are never in direct contact with each other on an e-mail system. It is important to emphasise this point. It is always an e-mail user who dials in to the central host computer, whether it is to check their mailbox or to send messages. An e-mail user never receives calls. For this reason an e-mail user does not have to be continuously connected to the system 'in case someone calls'.

Swapping messages via a central host computer overcomes many potential problems of incompatibility. E-mail users do not

14

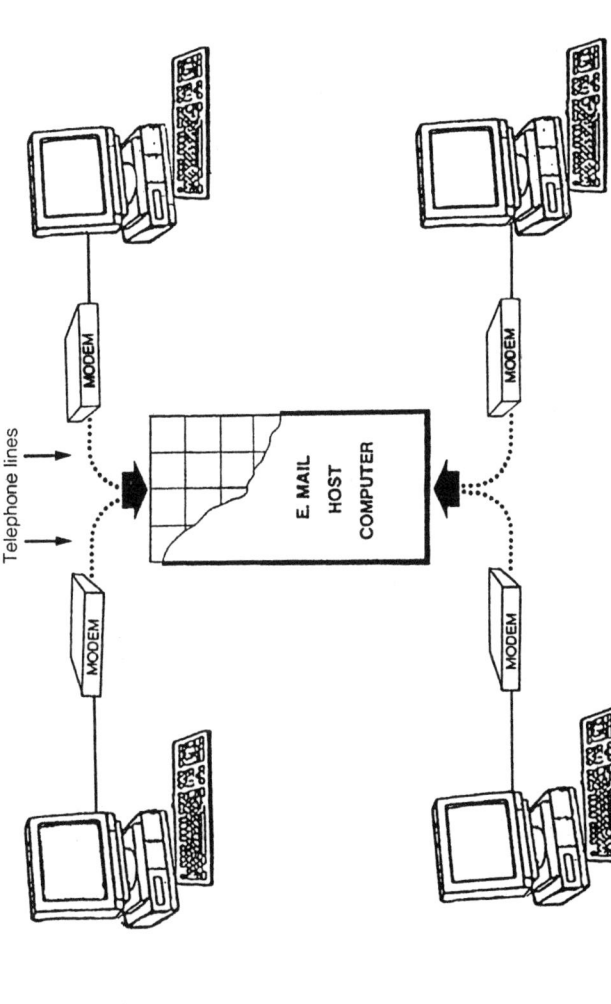

Figure 1: E-mail system E-mail members swap messages via the central host computer. Users are never in direct contact with each other.

need compatible computers or modems in order to communicate, provided that they can link up with the central host computer.

It is difficult to predict how long a user will spend on-line (connected to the central host computer) each day. This will depend on the volume of mail being sent and received and also on the speed of operation of the modem. As a rough guide, 15 minutes a day should be sufficient for average-to-heavy usage. Time spent on-line (connected to the central host computer) is time when the microcomputer and telephone line are not available for other tasks. At other times, however, they can be used as normal.

Some e-mail users will dial direct from their microcomputer to the central host computer. For others it may be cheaper to use a technique known as 'packet switching'. This is a special service for computer data transmission. Many telephone companies offer packet switching networks for computer users. The advantage of packet switching is that it may be cheaper than a direct call. Packet switching charges will normally be based on the price of a local call plus a small supplement. This can result in savings for e-mail users who cannot access the central host computer with a local call. In particular, packet switching can be economical on international calls. Packet switching is discussed in Chapter 7.

E-mail users will generally prepare messages on a word processor and save them on disc before connecting up with the central host computer. With the aid of a communications software package the messages can then be sent direct from disc to the central host computer where they are posted in the appropriate mailboxes. Sending a file direct from disc is known as 'uploading' a message. Similarly, e-mail users will not normally read new messages on screen. Instead they will capture them direct to disc for editing and printing at a later point. Capturing a message to disc is known as 'downloading' a file. E-mail users upload (send from disc) and download (capture to disc) because it is fast and convenient. Most e-mail systems have a scale of charges in part related to on-line time — that is to say the amount of time a member spends directly connected to the central host computer. Uploading and downloading messages saves time and therefore money.

16

Costs

E-mail often works out to be cheaper than telex or fax. However, the exact costs involved are complex and difficult to calculate. An e-mail user may have to pay a regular subscription to the e-mail system. In addition, most systems add a small charge for on-line time (time spent connected to the central host) above a certain threshold. For example, charges might be added for access over one hour per month. Sending fax or telex via the e-mail system, and access to most databases, will incur additional charges. The e-mail user will also have to pay normal telephone charges. If the e-mail subscriber uses the special system for data transmission called packet switching (see Chapter 7) then the telephone calls will probably only be charged at local rates. There will, however, be additional packet switching charges. These may consist of a regular standing charge plus a small charge both by time and by the amount of data transferred. International packet switching calls are charged at a separate rate.

These charges are, however, only half the story. It is important to remember that both the sender and the recipient pay for an e-mail transmission. The sender pays to post the message to the central host computer while the recipient pays the same charges to read the message. This is why 'junk' mail is unpopular on e-mail systems.

A sizable proportion of e-mail costs will be made up of fixed standing charges. Up to a point, therefore, the unit price per message will decrease with increased usage. It is virtually impossible, however, to calculate the exact cost of any one particular e-mail transmission.

Training

E-mail is complex to use, so training is vital. All too often, however, training in computerisation projects is inadequate or completely absent. Yet without proper training staff may quickly become frustrated and lose all confidence in the system.

It is far too easy for an organisation to fall into the trap of relying on one technically minded person to 'do the e-mail' but this can never be the basis for serious use of e-mail by an organisation. If e-mail is to make a contribution in an overall

17

communications strategy, then comprehensive staff training and good reference manuals are essential.

Advantages

Costs: As mentioned, e-mail is often a cheaper form of communication than telex or fax. E-mail via packet switching may be particularly attractive in developing countries where telex and international telephone costs are relatively high.

It is generally existing microcomputer users who are attracted to e-mail. Given that a computer has already been purchased, all that is normally needed to use e-mail is a modem, a communications software package and access to a phone line for a short period each day. There is only one major exception: it may not be possible to use e-mail on a telephone line going through a central switchboard. This will depend on the nature of the switchboard. In certain cases it may be necessary to have a direct phone line that does not go through the switchboard.

The capital costs of e-mail are small compared to the price of a telex terminal or a fax machine. A new telex may also necessitate the installation of an expensive new telex line. Except in cases of light usage, a fax machine will require a telephone line dedicated solely to fax. The use of e-mail, by contrast, does not normally require a dedicated phone line. In addition, the running costs of e-mail may be lower than fax and telex. In some cases e-mail will even be cheaper than the postal service.

The cost of sending multiple copies of a single message by e-mail will be little more than the cost of sending the message to one recipient. Once the text of a message has been transmitted to the host computer it is simple to place copies of the message in more than one mailbox. The benefits are obvious, for example in issuing a press release or circulating information to a network of partners. By contrast, circulating a message to, say, 30 partners using fax or telex would require paying for 30 individual transmissions.

International communications: E-mail can provide good worldwide communications and is feasible in many (but not all) countries. There has been a good take-up amongst NGOs and other local organisations in those developing countries where

18

e-mail is possible. Many organisations in the Third World have joined e-mail systems in developed countries. The London-based host of the GeoNet e-mail system, for example, has members in about 45 different countries. On the other hand, small, regional e-mail systems catering for local NGOs and similar organisations are beginning to appear in a number of developing countries. Such regional systems are already established in Brazil, Nicaragua, the Philippines, South Africa, Thailand and Uruguay. There is every reason to expect that this trend will continue.

An international message sent by e-mail is generally a good deal cheaper than a telex message. It may also be cheaper than fax. There are two reasons why e-mail is a relatively cheap form of international communication. Firstly, e-mail members may be able to connect up with the central host computer by using the technique known as packet switching. Packet switching is a special service for transmitting computer data. An international e-mail call via packet switching is a good deal cheaper than the equivalent international voice telephone call. Packet switching will, therefore, be of particular benefit to e-mail users based in a different country to the e-mail host computer. Packet switching is discussed in Chapter 7.

The second factor that can make e-mail a relatively cheap way to send international messages is the increasing number of regional e-mail systems, mentioned above. These systems are inter-linked and also linked to the larger international systems through a series of connections known as 'gateways' (see page 34). Gateways provide a cheap method of international communication. An international message can go 'island hopping' from e-mail system to e-mail system in order to get to its destination. The drawback is that the exchange of messages between different systems only occurs at certain times each day. It may take a couple of days for a message to arrive if it goes via several other systems.

To say that international e-mail is cheaper than telex or fax is not to say that international e-mail is cheap. The costs involved are still considerable. Nonetheless, for many organisations in the South effective communication with the international community is such a high priority that they are prepared to pay the price.

PART ONE: GENERAL

Networking: The possibility of sending cheap multiple copies and relatively cheap international messages can lead to tremendous savings in certain circumstances. The cost benefits of e-mail will be most apparent in situations such as the international exchange of information in partner networks. 'Networking' is discussed more fully in Chapter 2.

More important than savings on existing communications, however, is the fact that e-mail may actually encourage an exchange of information between partners. It can be a tool in the development of existing and new networks.

Message editing: A further feature of e-mail communication is that incoming messages can be captured to disc. Such messages can, if required, be edited in a word processing package and then re-sent. This will be of great benefit for any group of people working on a common text such as a newsletter or a joint report. Drafts can be edited and circulated without the need for the entire text to be re-typed.

It is also extremely useful for news and media organisations. It is quite normal in the commercial world for reporters to file their copy by electronic means.

Mobility: A subscriber is not tied to one particular location when using e-mail. Portable microcomputers are becoming increasingly common. These are briefcase-sized computers that can run off batteries. Models are available with an internal modem fitted inside the machine. With such a computer it is possible to use e-mail from any location — provided that there is access to a phone line for a short period. There is no obstacle to using e-mail from home or when visiting outside sites. There are many variations between the telephone systems of different countries. Experienced users, however, will often be able to send and read mail while travelling abroad.

Error correction: A final point about e-mail is that effective error correction techniques exist (see Chapter 6) which can guarantee the error free transmission of a message. Interference is not normally an issue for telex transmissions but it can be a big problem on international fax calls.

20

Disadvantages

Complex to use: As mentioned above, e-mail is a good deal more complex to use than telex or fax. Thorough staff training is essential. This requires time and money. By comparison, it is straightforward to introduce fax or telex into an organisation, as neither requires such extensive preparation.

Lack of immediacy: E-mail communication depends on the recipient regularly checking their mailbox — otherwise messages will just sit there unread. Various attempts have been made to overcome this potential problem. The most successful is probably 'receipt confirmation' messages. Using this facility, a short confirmation is automatically returned to the sender when a message is read by the recipient. In this way it is possible to keep track of messages and to follow them up if they have not been read. Nonetheless, e-mail is a form of communication that depends on the commitment of the recipient. This weakness is least evident in partner networks where all the participants have an active interest in the success of the network.

E-mail is not well-suited to unexpected, urgent communications. In such situations fax, telex or telephone are all preferable.

Complex costs: As outlined above, the calculation of the overall cost of e-mail will be based on a variety of different invoices. These may be mixed with charges for unrelated items, will arrive at different times, and may cover different periods. None of this is too much trouble for an individual or a small organisation. It is, however, a major problem in large organisations. Internal billing of different departments and budgetary forecasting for e-mail are a headache! The costs of telex, fax and direct computer to computer communications are, by contrast, relatively straightforward to calculate.

In addition, many e-mail users in developing countries belong to e-mail systems in developed countries. This means that e-mail is often more expensive for users in developing countries, who face higher telephone and packet switching charges, than it is for the rich Western agencies. One solution would be to have a split scale of charges whereby users in developed countries would pay higher charges and so subsidise Third World members. Another option would be for users in developed countries to pay the full e-mail system charges for the transmission of a message — in other words, pay when it is sent and when it is read. This would, however, cover only the e-mail system connection charges for Third World users — not their telephone or packet switching bills.

Risk of failure: In general, computers and modems are no less reliable than telex terminals or fax machines. Communication by e-mail, however, is more prone to failure than fax or telex because it is more complex. There is quite simply more that can go wrong.

Organisations that rely on the use of telex or fax will normally have some form of maintenance or rental agreement with the suppliers. If the equipment fails then, in the majority of cases, the organisation will call the engineers who will either fix or replace the equipment. The problem with e-mail is a lack of 'one-stop shopping'. There is not one single company or organisation that can take overall responsibility for the functioning of the system. Faults could develop with the computer or modem, the communications software, the packet switching system or the e-mail host computer. The people running an e-mail system will generally be very helpful in trying to diagnose the cause of problems. The responsibility for fixing them, however, may lie with some outside body such as a supplier, maintenance company or telephone company.

International calls can be particularly troublesome. A normal e-mail call from the Dominican Republic to London, for example, may be routed through Puerto Rico and the USA. When problems occur it can be difficult to determine the point of origin. There is a tendency for the different operators to decline responsibility and pass the buck to their counterparts.

To calculate the chance of an e-mail communication failing involves doubling all of the potential risk factors! Even if a subscriber manages to send a message to the central host computer successfully there is no guarantee that it will be read. The intended recipient may be suffering from hardware, software, telephone or packet switching problems.

TELECOMMUNICATIONS: AN OVERVIEW

No organisation should be foolish enough to rely on only one method of communication. This is particularly relevant for e-mail, especially when there is a need to transmit messages which are urgent or tied to deadlines. E-mail will fail from time to time. Even though the vast majority of failures will only be short-term, effective alternatives must be available.

Telex and fax via e-mail

Most e-mail systems allow subscribers to send fax or telex messages. The e-mail user will 'log on' (connect up) to the central host computer as usual. The text of the message is uploaded (sent) from the personal computer to the host in the normal way. The user will then issue commands indicating that a fax or telex is to be sent to a specified number. The central host computer will regulate the necessary conversions and then forward the message, which will be received at its destination as a normal telex or fax.

Similarly, it is possible to receive a telex message in a mailbox on an e-mail system. The telex must be sent to the telex number of the e-mail system with the first line of the telex message identifying the mailbox name of the e-mail subscriber. The host computer scans the first line of the telex and automatically places the text in the appropriate mailbox. The recipient will find the telex message the next time they check their mailbox. Alternatively, it may be possible for an e-mail user to rent a personal telex number from the e-mail company. Telex messages received on a personal telex number are automatically placed in the appropriate mailbox. It is not necessary for the telex message to quote the mailbox name of the recipient.

Fax can be sent by e-mail users along the same lines as telex messages. It is also possible for e-mail users to receive fax but this area is still under development. The difficulty is that fax transmissions may include graphics or handwritten text while normal e-mail messages are entirely text-based, though this is likely to be solved in the next few years.

The main advantage of sending fax and telex via e-mail is that users gain access to telex and fax facilities without the high initial outlay required to obtain a fax or telex machine. The facility would be most useful for organisations that occasionally send telex or fax but cannot justify the capital cost of installing a dedicated machine. There is, however, a surcharge for each telex or fax that is sent via e-mail. In some circumstances this will mean that it will cost more to send a telex or fax via e-mail than from a proper fax or telex machine. Nonetheless, it is worth noting that in many developing countries, and some developed countries, telex charges are very high — maybe considerably higher than the telex charges in the country in which the e-mail host computer is based. In this case it will still be cheaper to send a telex via e-mail even if it is possible to get access to a proper telex terminal in the country of origin.

One argument in favour of fax or telex is that far more individuals and organisations use these technologies than use e-mail. It is, however, possible to send messages to fax and telex users via e-mail. At the moment it is not possible to receive fax to an e-mail system but this should change within the coming years. The main drawback of receiving fax and telex via e-mail is that incoming messages must include the mailbox name of the recipient in the first line, except in the case of personal telex numbers. This is fine for partners that are known to one another but may cause problems for senders unfamiliar with the workings of the e-mail system. Telex or fax that do not include the mailbox name may not find their way to the right destination.

E-mail 2

The first chapter considered e-mail alongside other forms of telecommunications. This chapter concentrates on e-mail and examines the ways in which it may aid the work of non-commercial organisations.

Networking

Networking implies the coming together of organisations on an equal basis for the purpose of sharing resources and information. Networking is of particular interest to NGOs, charities, campaigning groups and similar bodies, where receiving and disseminating information is an essential part of their work. Research workers and journalists are natural participants in the networks that spring up around such groups.

Of course networking is nothing new. It has gone on by post and by phone for years. It is also possible to maintain a network of contacts by fax but this is expensive and may be inconvenient. E-mail is attractive because it is particularly well-suited to the development of networks. Information circulated on a network is often important but not confined to a deadline, and participants are generally committed to the success of the system. In such situations the potential drawbacks of e-mail — lack of immediacy, risk of failure, etc — are minimised, while the strengths of e-mail — good international communication, cheap broadcast to multiple destinations, etc — are maximised. E-mail fits naturally into this kind of work. It not only supports established channels of information exchange by improving communication, but can also stimulate the expansion of existing networks and the development of new patterns of communication.

Already in existence are some large, well-established,

international networks such as Huridocs, the human rights network, and Satis, the global network of organisations working with technologies for sustainable development. (There is more information on these and other networks in Chapter Three.) Such large networks have a fairly stable structure with defined membership criteria and mechanisms for decision-making and participation. The member organisations will generally know and trust each other. They will be prepared to make commitments to their partners and to work towards agreed goals. It can be said with certainty that e-mail will play an increasingly important role in the development of these networks.

Besides the general benefits that networking offers, these larger associations play a valuable role in developing 'standards' for storing and requesting information. Both Huridocs and Satis have developed classification systems suitable for their areas of work. The same standards can be applied to both computerised and manual information systems. Developing a common classification system is a vital prerequisite for improving the flow of information between different organisations.

In addition to the larger networks, 'mini networks' spring up quite spontaneously on existing e-mail systems. They are based around the bulletin boards and mailing lists provided by the e-mail systems (see page 29). These small networks are more loose-knit and volatile than their larger counterparts. They act as a channel for distributing information on a certain subject rather than as a platform for joint development or common action. There are no membership requirements and the participants have no mutual obligations.

Networking is a 'way of life' rather than an abstract theory of communication. It entails the constant interchange of information between peers and so a constant alertness to that which will be useful for oneself or for others. In this connection, it has frequently been noted that e-mail tends to encourage forms of communication which are less formal than those carried on through traditional channels. People who have never met one another adopt a relaxed tone in e-mail messages that might be absent in ordinary letters.

Some problems associated with Information Technology

It should not be imagined that the spread of information technology is without problems. Overworked staff in many western NGOs, for example, could be forgiven for fearing that more and faster information will not particularly help them in their work. Already — in the developed world at least — we are flooded with newsletters, reports, magazines and so forth. It is clear that the problem is not how to get information, or how to get more information, but how to get the right information. In the short-term e-mail will certainly only add to the general flow of information. However, the longer-term significance of this increased availability of information and the spread of e-mail must be viewed in the light of other expected developments. Organisations entering this new 'Age of Information' will have to accommodate new problems and new challenges.

One response to the increasing flood of information is the growth of documentation and resource centres with staff trained in the techniques of information technology. The coming years may also witness the development of new types of independent organisations dealing specifically with information. Acting as mediators or 'information brokers', such bodies will have the specific aim of getting the right information to the right people at the right time. The development of appropriate, on-line NGO databases will also be of tremendous importance in harnessing the power of information technology for the non-commercial sector. Using these databases it is far easier to pinpoint relevant material from the mass of information available. One such database is examined in more detail below (see page 33).

The spread of information technology may also impede the functioning of partner network since more and faster information is by no means the same as better quality information. Irrelevant material can clog the system and cause members to lose faith in its value. The real challenge of networking is to encourage the exchange of useful information between partners. It is, therefore, essential that participants know something about each other's projects and aims. If urgent calls for action are broadcast on a network then activists must not only know one another but must also share some degree of mutual trust and mutual obligation. Formal or informal bonds must exist if established procedures for internal deliberation and consultation are to be accelerated or skipped. Regular, for example annual, meetings of partners can play a vital role in fostering understanding and a sense of trust between participants. Such meetings are important in strengthening and expanding the functioning of a network. They can indirectly assist in reducing information overdose by helping organisations to discover what is useful for their partners.

'Closed' user groups

The idea of a 'closed user group' is related to the network model but it refers to a group of users who subscribe to an e-mail network specifically to improve communications between one another. It is rather like a private network since the members are not primarily interested in communicating with organisations outside the group. A closed group might be formed by different departments or separate offices within an organisation. A development organisation with several overseas offices is a typical example.

The main aim of the closed group is to provide efficient and relatively cheap internal communications. Any benefits resulting from improved communications with outside groups are simply an added bonus. Internal communications, such as memos and reports, can be circulated very cheaply. This is both because e-mail is a relatively cheap form of international communications and because the charge for sending multiple copies is virtually the same as the charge for sending a single copy. The flow of internal information can be improved and the participation of regional offices in central decision-making can be encouraged.

There is one further benefit which may be of great importance: an improvement in the 'lateral' communications between offices. It is frequently the case with more traditional forms of communication that there is little direct exchange of information between the 'peripheral' offices. An office in Latin America and another in Africa, for example, might communicate with London.

28

There is often little direct contact or sharing of experience between the regional centres. Using e-mail, however, the office in Latin America and the office in Africa can easily communicate with each other, provided that they can both establish a reasonable link with the central host computer of the e-mail system. The possibility of improved lateral communications is often an exciting prospect for workers in regional offices. The centre, however, is sometimes less enthusiastic about the idea of increasing the power of the periphery!

E-mail systems in general

E-mail systems offer a number of facilities that can aid networking and the interchange of information between partners or within closed user groups. The following pages describe some of the features common to non-commercial e-mail systems, such as bulletin boards, mailing lists and gateways. This section also includes entries on the use of e-mail from developing countries, small systems and security.

Bulletin boards, conferences and mailing lists
Bulletin boards and mailing lists are two facilities available on e-mail systems that aid networking. On some systems 'bulletin boards' are known as 'conferences'.

In its simplest form, the idea of the bulletin board or conference is that any member of the e-mail system can post a message in a public area. Any other member of the system can browse through the bulletin boards reading items of interest. A brief summary of the contents is attached to each message. It is therefore unnecessary to read every message on a bulletin board in order to find relevant items. As a first step, the user simply scans the summaries. E-mail systems offer a variety of bulletin boards divided by geographical region or subject: Latin America, Southern Africa and environmental issues are examples. It is possible for users to attach comments to the articles posted by other subscribers on a bulletin board. All e-mail networks offer some method of identifying which bulletin boards have had new

```
Command: check labour

(LABOUR) Command: scan 13-06-90

No.  * Date  Time  From/To      Lines  Subject

16   8 28-06 17:18 ILR            49   INTERNATIONAL LABOUR REPORTS 40
24   4 14-06 09:52 ICEF-BRU       51   INFO:VENEZUELAN BARGAINING
25   4 22-06 14:22 CIC           212   CHINA: WORKERS DETAINED - BEIJING
27   3 05-07 05:25 AMRC           61   TAIWAN: SOLIDARITY CALL
28   5 06-07 08:12 GN            170   EL SALVADOR/LABOR RIGHTS
29   4 06-07 15:39 ICEF-BRU      302   INFO:NEW SAFETY NORMS
83   5 14-06 09:56 ICEF-BRU       62   INFO:BRAZIL SOLVAY STRIKE
86   6 14-06 10:06 ICEF-BRU       62   INFO:UNIONISTS MURDERED
87   4 14-06 20:11 ELSSOC         57   HONDURAN TRADE UNIONISTS MURDERED
88  10 15-06 10:07 KRIG           17   NEW ADDRESS AND PHONE OF KRIC
89   6 15-06 15:59 ICEF-BRU       71   INFO:ILO ENVIRONMENT ROLE
90   9 18-06 09:55 AMRC           31   1992 : SOME RESOURCES
91   3 22-06 14:30 CIC            80   CHINA: WORKERS DETAINED - CHANGSHA
95  13 25-06 06:23 AMRC           94   WRITER/EDITOR WANTED
96   7 28-06 10:04 GN             48   INTERNATIONAL CALL-IN SUPPORT PICO
97  12 29-06 10:36 MALCHEM        17   FLEXI-WAGE SYSTEM.CAN YOU HELP US

(LABOUR) Command:
```

Figure 2: *Bulletin board* The screen shows a number of entries posted on a typical GeoNet bulletin board. The information displayed includes: the message number, the number of times the message has been read, the date and time the message was posted, the organisation which posted the message, the number of lines, and a brief description of the contents.

items added to them since they were last visited by a user or since a given date. It is therefore not necessary to check all the bulletin boards but only the ones with new messages.

There are a number of variations on this basic system. The right to post messages on a board may, for example, be restricted to specific organisations or individuals (although anyone can read the board). In this way a certain standard and outlook can be ensured by the people who run the board. A variant is that users may be charged for inspecting a bulletin board — possibly one offering commercial or specialist services. Before entering such a board, subscribers will receive a message warning that there is a charge for access. A third variation is that a bulletin board may only be available to a specific 'closed' group of users. A password is required to gain access to such a bulletin board. A private bulletin board might be used by a small circle of users such as an editorial panel or a steering committee. Such boards are also established by some organisations for use only by their members. They can be a useful forum for developing ideas and pursuing internal debates.

The public areas on the e-mail systems which come under the umbrella of the Association for Progressive Communications (APC) are known as 'conferences'. The principle is exactly the same as the bulletin board but the actual operation is a little different. On the APC systems a conference is divided into different topics. Any topic may have a series of comments attached to it by participants in the discussion. These comments will not be visible unless a given topic is entered.

Bulletin boards are geared towards the simple posting of information. Comments are treated as new items of information and will be seen by everyone who visits the bulletin board. Conferences, on the other hand, encourage participation and a rather more discursive style since comments are only seen by a smaller group of users. Both systems have advantages and disadvantages.

At their best, bulletin boards are great fun. They can be a valuable source of information and contacts on a given subject. The benefits for networking are obvious. Bulletin boards are regularly used to broadcast appeals and press releases, to circulate requests for information, to publicise forthcoming actions, and

31

as a forum for the on-going exchange of information on given topics. In addition, some bulletin boards carry high quality 'on-line' magazines. For example, an organisation based in Zimbabwe called Africa Information Afrique produces a series of regular news updates from Southern Africa. These are available, free of charge, to all users of bulletin boards and conferences on several e-mail systems.

As the use of e-mail — and users' sophistication — increases, the short-comings of the bulletin board system also become more apparent. In particular, it is time-consuming to monitor a range of bulletin boards, especially when many new articles posted on a given board may not be of relevance to a particular user. An organisation interested in women's issues, for example, might find itself monitoring a wide range of bulletin boards dedicated to different geographical regions, simply because relevant articles are sometimes posted on them. These considerations have, in part, prompted the development of NGO databases, such as the Nigel system described below.

As well as the bulletin boards and conferences available on largish e-mail systems, there are countless individual bulletin boards run by enthusiasts simply for fun. These individual bulletin boards are not a part of a larger e-mail system but are located on private personal computers. The system operator, or SysOp, will make the bulletin board available to all-comers on a private phone line for part or all of the day. Access to these systems is achieved by a computer phone call direct to the private number of the SysOp. There are private bulletin boards specialising in every conceivable topic, from Christian awareness to hacking. Details of these boards circulate privately amongst enthusiasts and in specialist publications. They do not fall within the scope of this book.

In several developing countries systems catering specifically for NGOs have emerged. These systems are something between specialist bulletin boards and small e-mail systems. They are described later in this chapter (see page 35).

The second tool for networking offered by e-mail systems is the 'mailing list', which is simply a collection of organisations interested in a certain topic. A mailing list consists of the mailbox names of other members of the system and may, in certain circumstances, also include the mailbox names of users of different systems. In addition, it can include telex or fax numbers for organisations that do not use e-mail. A mailing list might, for example, be called BRAZIL. Any message sent to the mailing list BRAZIL will be received automatically by all participants either as an e-mail message, a telex or a fax. Such a system is a useful means of efficiently broadcasting press releases, general announcements and the like.

The e-mail systems grouped under the umbrella of the Association for Progressive Communications (APC) offer a similar feature known as the user list. This allows a system member to extract a list of mailbox names based on certain keywords. A search on 'rainforest', for example, will produce a list of all users who have recorded an interest in this field. This may be a list for one particular e-mail system or for all the systems on the APC network.

NGO databases: Nigel

The importance of the development of on-line NGO databases for the non-commercial sector has already been mentioned (see page 27). One such database, currently being developed by Antenna in conjunction with the GeoNet and GreenNet e-mail systems, is called Nigel. The Nigel database operates along lines that will be entirely familiar to users of normal, commercial databases. It is of interest to non-commercial users because it specialises in information to and from NGOs and because the access charges are a fraction of those for normal, commercial databases.

Users of Nigel need only specify key words for their searches and are then presented with a 'set' that lists all the relevant items in the database. It is possible to further refine a given set by specifying additional key words or by applying a date filter, so that, for example, only items posted after a certain date are included. Users can scan a summary of the items in a set or download them (copy to disc) for editing and printing at a later point.

Nigel offers great benefits for information providers and information seekers alike. Information providers can make their material available to a wider potential audience. If desired, a charge can be levied each time material in the database is accessed.

This will ensure that potential income from the sale of normal printed publications is not lost. Information seekers, on the other hand, find it far easier to pinpoint relevant information. The bulletin board is still the best medium for browsing and exchanging general information. The database, however, is a far more efficient tool for those users with a specific interest in, for example, all articles on Zimbabwe or Korean unions.

In its pilot version, the Nigel database has been used for a wide variety of different applications. It can provide a directory of all e-mail users on several different systems indexed by region, area of interest etc. There is also a catalogue (indexed by organisation, subject material etc) of all 1,600 publications available through the Satis network of organisations working for sustainable development. A third database offers a fully indexed archive of back issues of various on-line publications, such as the Southscan magazine.

Gateways

A gateway is a link between two separate e-mail systems. It allows members of different systems to swap messages with the minimum of fuss. The gateways on non-commercial systems are semi-, rather than fully, automatic. Messages for a remote system are stored up on the home system. The remote system is periodically dialled up and all incoming and outgoing mail is swapped. A message to a user on a remote system will not be delivered instantaneously. It will sit around on the home system until the next time the gateway is opened. The gateways between the main progressive e-mail systems are opened several times each day. For data exchange between e-mail systems the operators use special high-speed connections in order to keep costs to a minimum.

Gateways are an important element in the success of non-commercial e-mail networks. They allow small, 'appropriate' local e-mail systems to thrive. Gateways allow the users on these small systems to swap messages with partners on different systems around the world. Non-commercial systems normally give a high priority to providing good gateways with other systems. This fits in with their general philosophy of encouraging cooperation and communication between all non-commercial users.

There is a company in the United States called Dasnet which can swap messages between most e-mail systems where gateways do not exist. Dasnet can be useful for 'one-off' correspondence with a user on a different system but it would be expensive to use on a regular basis.

Small systems
An increasingly popular trend is the creation of regional e-mail systems with a small host computer based in a developing country. There are, for example, small independent systems in the Philippines, South Africa, Thailand, and Uruguay with similar plans for Zimbabwe and Kenya. In passing it is worth mentioning that a small e-mail system along these lines has also been started in Estonia.

Most small systems are not joined directly to a packet switching network (see Chapter 7). Packet switching is a system for the cheap and efficient transmission of computer data. A host computer must be quite sophisticated if it is to be linked in to a packet switching network. Instead of using packet switching, the small systems establish gateways with larger, international e-mail systems using high speed modems. At regular, often daily, intervals, the small systems dial in to the larger systems to swap incoming and outgoing messages. In this way members are able to communicate with users on other systems. This approach keeps down the cost of international calls without requiring sophisticated computer equipment.

E-mail in developing countries
Readers in developing countries will already know all about their own local facilities. This short section is aimed primarily at readers who may be wondering whether their overseas offices or partners in the South might be able to use e-mail.

In the first instance the use of e-mail will, of course, depend on the general local computer situation. Much of the South is currently experiencing a boom in the use of microcomputers. Problems of service and supply are slowly disappearing. Nonetheless, in many countries the success of a computer project

35

still depends on the availability of local expertise and reliable suppliers.

It should normally be possible to use e-mail in a developing country if that country offers packet switching. Packet switching is a facility provided by telecommunications companies which makes the sending of computer data easier and cheaper (see Chapter 7). The fact that a country offers packet switching is in itself a fair indicator that other conditions are far enough developed for the use of e-mail. If packet switching is not on offer then it will probably be necessary to use the packet switching system in a neighbouring country. This involves placing international calls to the neighbouring country and will increase both costs and bureaucratic problems. It may also be possible to connect up with the central host computer through a direct international telephone call. This will, however, increase the running costs of e-mail.

As mentioned, some countries in the South have developed small NGO e-mail networks that have gateways to larger outside systems. In these cases any problems arising from lack of packet switching will not be relevant. Normally, however, e-mail will be a tricky proposition if local packet switching is not available.

E-mail should be feasible from most countries in Central and South America. The situation in Latin America should continue to improve with plans for new regional e-mail systems under development. Packet switching is also available from many countries in the Far East and it has recently been introduced in India.

Countries in southern Africa may be able to use the South African packet switching system. E-mail is, for example, possible from Namibia. Zimbabwe has its own packet switching system but it is rather difficult to get access to it. In the rest of Africa, with the possible exception of Senegal and neighbouring Francophone countries, e-mail is currently problematic. The development of small regional e-mail systems may, however, have a dramatic impact on this picture. There is already a flourishing NGO e-mail system in South Africa with similar systems under development in Zimbabwe and Kenya. Work is also under way to provide efficient automatic gateways with GeoNet or GreenNet in England (it costs less for these systems to communicate individually with London than with each other). There is tremendous scope for further development, should these small African e-mail systems prove successful.

E-mail from developing countries is not cheap. It will generally be used by organisations rather than by individuals. The costs, however, must normally be judged in relation to the costs and problems of other methods of communication. For some organisations the ability to establish fast and reliable communications with the international community is worth a great deal.

Security

Under normal circumstances, communication by e-mail is no more secure than an ordinary telephone call. There is no reason why the telephone line which the subscriber uses for e-mail cannot be tapped. Messages can then easily be 'read' by the tapper when the e-mail user checks his or her mailbox. The same, incidentally, is true of fax.

It is possible to develop reasonably secure methods for transmitting information but it requires care and planning. The messages can, for example, be coded, provided that there is prior agreement between the sender and the receiver. It is also possible to use a portable computer to send and read mail from a variety of different telephone numbers. For normal use, however, e-mail is not a secure form of communication. This in no way negates its usefulness for transmitting material which is not of a sensitive nature.

E-mail systems in particular

Non-commercial users of e-mail tend to congregate on certain systems. These are not normally the large commercial e-mail systems, but may be non-commercial networks or systems that in some way attract non-commercial and small users. Most non-commercial users do not need to use e-mail to communicate with those companies and businesses on the large systems. They can do this perfectly well by other means, such as post, fax or telephone.

PART ONE: GENERAL

The distinct advantages that e-mail offers — networking and the open exchange of information — do not demand large systems. They simply require that all like-minded organisations belong to similar systems. In this respect, the non-commercial sector forms a well-defined user community that belongs to a well-defined set of smaller e-mail systems. In broad terms, the e-mail systems used by non-commercial organisations can be separated into two groups.

On the one hand there is a set of seven different systems grouped together under the umbrella of the Association for Progressive Communications (APC). These systems are: Alternex in Brazil, GreenNet in Britain, the Institute for Global Communications (IGC) in the USA, Nicarao in Nicaragua, PeaceNet Sweden, Pegasus in Australia and the Web in Canada. The Institute for Global Communications (IGC), which is based in San Francisco, runs a computer that plays host to four different networks. These are: PeaceNet, EcoNet, ConflictNet and HomeoNet. To an e-mail user these networks appear as separate APC e-mail systems. All the mailboxes of PeaceNet and EcoNet users are in fact physically situated on the host which is run by IGC. Most of the ConflictNet and HomeoNet users are also situated on this host although there are some users who are situated on other APC e-mail systems such as GreenNet. All of the APC systems are non-profit systems. They run on similar types of computer. There are excellent gateways between all of the different systems. It is a simple matter to send mail to users on other systems. APC conferences are automatically updated with material from the conferences on other systems. Many types of non-commercial users subscribe to APC systems. There is, however, a preponderance of peace and environmental groups.

The other main camp is the GeoMail community. GeoMail is a commercial system of West German origin. It consists of an association of a number of separate GeoNet host computers run by individual operators. Most of the host computers are situated in different European countries but there is one in the USA. Again, the different hosts are linked together so that communication between them is a simple matter. There is a GeoNet host in Britain that specialises in providing services for non-commercial organisations. The GeoMail system is run for profit but its administration is sympathetic to the idea of providing a service for non-commercial users. About 600 subscribers from around 45 countries have mailboxes on the GeoNet host in Britain which is administered by a group called Poptel. These include many types of organisations but with a bias towards the labour, cooperative and development movements.

Besides these two main groups there are other e-mail systems which may be of interest to NGO users. *MCI Mail*, for example, is a major commercial e-mail system based in the USA. It is reasonably priced and has a broad spectrum of users including development workers and journalists. The system has many users in the USA but does not have a high profile in Europe. The *Telecommunications Cooperative Network (TCN)* is an e-mail system established on the Dialcom telecommunications system in New York. TCN has links with various United Nations bodies but does not have many active NGO users. *EIES* is the short name given to the Electronic Information Exchange System based in the New Jersey Institute of Technology. Members of this e-mail system are mostly based in the US and Latin America. EIES has a mixture of NGO and other users. *JANET* is a British system which links many different computers in universities, polytechnics and other research establishments. It is the main academic network in Britain. *Telecom* or *Dialcom Gold* is a large commercial e-mail system based in the UK. It is a relatively expensive system which does not hold any particular attraction for non-commercial users.

Fidonet is different from the other systems mentioned here. Fido is the name of a popular software package used to run private bulletin boards. These individual bulletin boards are run by enthusiasts, often on a phone line from a private house. Some of the small e-mail systems in developing countries, referred to elsewhere in this book (see page 35), use Fido software. A feature of Fido software is that individual bulletin board operators can agree to a regular automated exchange of messages between their systems. Private operators agree these connections as it suits them. This results in a web of linked Fido bulletin boards spanning countries and continents. This is collectively known as Fidonet.

PART ONE: GENERAL

Poptel/GeoNet and GreenNet

The GeoNet host for non-commercial users is run by a London-based group called Poptel. There is a second London-based e-mail system called GreenNet. GreenNet belongs to the Association for Progressive Communications (APC). In January 1990 it was announced that Poptel and the administration of GreenNet would merge and form a single cooperative called Soft Solution. GreenNet and Poptel/GeoNet continue to exist as separate e-mail systems and are still run on separate host computers, but they are now located at the same site. The new cooperative has assumed responsibility for the running costs, administration and development of both systems.

This initiative has resulted in the pooling, rather than duplication, of scarce resources, while joint development will lead to far closer integration between the two systems. The existing gateway between Poptel/GeoNet and GreenNet will certainly be improved giving even better links between users on different systems. There is also the prospect of joint bulletin boards and conferences while the NGO database, Nigel, is now being developed for both GeoNet and GreenNet.

GeoNet and GreenNet are also collaborating with a number of other systems in the development of new gateways. These include a gateway to the Fido network and gateways to several small systems in Asia and Africa. The system run by the new body, Soft Solution, will act as a strong bridge between the APC and GeoMail systems. As a result, e-mail users will, hopefully, get the best of both worlds.

Case studies 3

This chapter contains eight case studies of organisations or networks in order to give an impression of the kinds of groups that use e-mail and the ways in which it is used. Each case study begins with a general description of the organisation or network before examining the specific ways in which it is using e-mail.

Contact details for the organisations and networks included in this chapter can be found in Appendix C.

Asia Monitor Resource Centre (AMRC)

A resource centre concentrating on labour issues in South, East, and South East Asia, AMRC is based in Hong Kong. It provides information services for workers' groups, trade unions and related organisations in South, East, and South East Asia. These information services include research, publishing, training and documentation, and focus on: occupational health and safety; transnational corporations and economic analysis of industrial sectors; labour movements and organisations; labour conditions; labour laws; and the use of new information technology for trade unions and NGOs.

AMRC has undertaken projects in many Asian countries to equip and train NGOs and trade unions in the use of computer communications. It also provides demonstrations, consultancy, written information and training materials relating to new information technology as part of its general information work. It seeks to encourage international grassroots links between organisations concerned with issues that affect workers. Organisations in industrial countries, for example, often provide information on occupational health or economic issues while Asian organisations generally provide details of labour conditions, the trade union movement or contact addresses.

41

PART ONE: GENERAL

E-mail: AMRC is a long-established and experienced user of e-mail. It uses e-mail to communicate with trade unions, new technology groups, funders, visitors and NGOs working in relevant fields, sending and receiving a wide variety of messages. These include requests for information; emergency appeals and solidarity or protest statements; arrangements for visits and conferences (often at short notice); articles for publication; and administrative correspondence with funders. E-mail is also used to communicate with staff travelling abroad. AMRC also participates in relevant bulletin boards or conferences on the GeoNet and APC e-mail systems. This involves posting articles and analyses, commenting on messages and responding to requests for information.

As part of its information services, AMRC interrogates commercial databases for business information on companies, general economic analyses, occupational health and safety, and chemical hazards. Newspaper and magazine databases provide additional information in the fields of labour news and politics. Due to its broad experience in the field, AMRC is well placed to highlight the drawbacks of e-mail. The work of AMRC indicates that the costs of e-mail remain high, especially when transmitting large volumes of data. With e-mail systems based in the North, Europeans get a cheaper service than Third World users, while all users still have to pay to read messages. Different e-mail systems and databases remain incompatible, adding to costs and multiplying invoices. E-mail remains complex to install and operate when compared to fax. It is complicated to send non-Latin scripts such as Chinese, Korean and Hindi.

Friends of the Earth

Friends of the Earth is one of the leading environmental pressure groups in the UK. At a national level, FoE UK campaigns on issues such as water pollution and toxics, energy, cities for people, re-cycling, air pollution, countryside and agriculture, tropical rainforests, and global warming. It pursues these campaigns through political lobbying and PR work, by commissioning

42

research and producing information material. At a local level, FoE has a network of more than 270 autonomous groups, which lobby local politicians and participate in national campaigns. At an international level, there are more than 35 national groups. These constitutionally independent organisations are brought together in the Friends of the Earth International network. Their activities are coordinated through the Friends of the Earth International Secretariat, currently based within the offices of FoE UK. The International Secretariat plays an important role in facilitating information exchange, joint campaigning and cooperative fundraising, and produces an international newsletter called FOE-Link.

E-mail: Friends of the Earth circulates minutes, agendas and other material for international meetings by e-mail. FOE-Link, the bi-monthly international newsletter, is available to paying subscribers either as printed copy or via e-mail. E-mail is a useful tool in some FoE campaigns but not in others. The tropical rainforest campaign involves extensive international exchange and here e-mail does have a role to play. FoE also uses e-mail for general information exchange, posting press releases on APC conferences (such as GreenNet and PeaceNet). These conferences are scanned for material relevant to FoE activists or researchers.

GreenNet is used heavily by some FoE UK local groups but is not in widespread general use at the local level. A potential danger in the increased use of e-mail is that it might encourage the development of a 'star' shaped network in which the smaller, local groups tend to relate individually to the larger FoE UK offices in London. Plans to increase the use of e-mail by local groups will, therefore, be within the context of developing broader, appropriate systems to encourage the decentralised exchange of information between peers at the regional and local levels.

Global Dialog Association (GDA)

The Global Dialog Association promotes data exchange and conferencing between the USSR, the USA, West Europe and

43

Japan. It is a new international NGO which aims at the global pooling of intellectual resources in order to resolve current problems in the economic, scientific, cultural and social spheres. It seeks to encourage worldwide dialogue and to organise the exchange of information by means of international data networks, television and interactive video, the press and other media. International e-mail is an important tool in achieving these aims. GDA and its member organisations use a wide range of e-mail systems, including GeoNet, Dialcom/Telecom Gold and the EIES system.

Many of the organisations mentioned in this book work with North-South dialogue. GDA, however, concentrates on facilitating information exchange between the USSR, the USA, West Europe and Japan. In the past there has been little precedent for East-West computer communications. GDA aims to provide a framework for the development of these links.

The head office of GDA is in France but it also has offices in the USSR, the USA and Japan. Honorary founder members of GDA include the Novosti Press Agency and the Institute of Sociology of the Academy of Sciences. There are also a number of information systems and e-mail networks based in the USA, Western Europe and Japan.

A first step in promoting these links is the development of internal computer communications within the USSR and also with other countries and systems. To this end, GDA is installing a host computer of the GeoNet e-mail system in its offices in Moscow. This will enable users in Moscow and other parts of the Soviet Union to use the GeoNet system on a similar basis to users in other Western European countries and the USA. It is intended that the Moscow host should offer maximum inter-connection with other services and systems in the USSR and the rest of the world.

Huridocs (Human Rights Information and Documentation Systems)

Huridocs is a decentralised, global network of human rights organisations. Its aim is to improve access to, and dissemination

44

of, public information on human rights. It does this by encouraging the adoption of effective, appropriate and compatible methods and techniques for information handling in the field of human rights. Huridocs works on the basis of a broad definition of human rights, including civil and political rights as well as economic, social and cultural rights. The network does not itself collect documentation. Instead it seeks to establish a decentralised network of organisations concerned with human rights information and documentation.

The network was formed in 1982. It has a small secretariat based in Norway. One of the most important aims of the network is the development of the Huridocs Standard Formats for Recording and Exchange of Information. These are a series of detailed recommendations relating to the handling of human rights information. The Huridocs classification system is suitable for both computerised and manual systems. It is used by many of its member organisations and other resource centres around the world.

The network is also active in organising training programmes relating to the principles of information handling and the use of the Huridocs Standard Formats. These courses normally contain modules relating to computers and the use of e-mail.

The work of Huridocs concentrates primarily on strengthening the information handling capacity of human rights organisations in developing countries. Most of its training courses are, therefore, either held in the South or are intended for participants from the South.

E-mail: The information exchanged on the network relates mostly to the planning and execution of Huridocs activities, information regarding its publications and computer programs etc. E-mail is used mostly for communication with organisations in developing countries, as it is here that speed and cost advantages are most obvious. Huridocs also uses e-mail to co-ordinate decision-making regarding its programme and activities. Members of its executive committee are located in various countries worldwide. Some of these, together with Huridocs technical consultants, use e-mail. There are plans to bring other 'core members' on-line.

Problems experienced by the Huridocs network include the lack of an e-mail training manual and difficulties in gaining access to the e-mail system by members when travelling abroad. In addition, the lack of packet switching in some developing countries has made it difficult for some members to connect to e-mail systems. In general, however, Huridocs is 'strongly committed' to encouraging and developing the use of e-mail.

IBASE (Instituto Brasileiro de Análises Sociais e Econômicas)

IBASE is a non-profit computer consultancy and research NGO based in Brazil and founded in 1981. It runs the Alternex e-mail system and provides studies, consultancy, data processing, data communications and other services to rural and urban workers' unions, community organisations, popular education and documentation centres, students and others. It is based in Rio but works with groups and other NGOs throughout Brazil and abroad. IBASE receives requests related to the following:

- studies on the social, political and economic situation of specific areas;
- studies to support alternative proposals to official policies;
- production and circulation of audiovisual and printed materials for training and popular education;
- data communications and data processing services;
- surveys;
- support for seminars and workshops.

IBASE has closely followed the microcomputer revolution and today has a network of more than 25 microcomputers. The Institute provides services such as databases, desktop publishing, statistical analyses and data processing of surveys.

E-Mail: Since early 1989, IBASE has been running the Alternex e-mail system in Brazil. Alternex is one of the seven e-mail systems grouped together under the umbrella of the Association for Progressive Communications (APC). The system is connected to the Brazilian packet switching system and is also accessible via a direct phone line. Alternex has been growing rapidly and by early 1990 there were already about 250 members of the system. It is noticeable that a large proportion of Alternex users are drawn from other countries in Latin America (Chile, Peru, Uruguay, Colombia). There are also users from Italy and Japan. In comparison to the overall growth of the system, the take-up amongst Brazilian users has been slow. One possible reason for this is a lack of resources for microcomputers and phone lines (which must be purchased and are expensive in Brazil). To counter this IBASE, together with other NGOs, is investigating the possibility of establishing 'community e-mail centres' in various large towns. These would be equipped with microcomputer, printer and modem and would be available to smaller community groups.

In addition to its ongoing work with the Alternex e-mail system, IBASE has also designed a database system on AIDS which can be accessed via the packet switching system. It holds information on hospitals, treatment methods, prevention etc. This project was developed in conjunction with the Brazilian Interdisciplinary AIDS Association.

IBASE itself makes intense use of e-mail in the course of its work. Staff use e-mail to exchange papers, proposals, studies, projects etc with counterparts within and outside Brazil. In addition, several members of the IBASE staff act as facilitators for other groups in Brazil who do not, as yet, have access to microcomputers. These groups exchange messages using the facilities at the offices of IBASE.

Interdoc

Interdoc is an information technology and e-mail network, describing itself as 'an informal network of NGOs, and networks of NGOs, established to facilitate the adoption and adaption of appropriate information handling techniques in order to permit the better delivery of services to their constituents'.

Since its formation in 1984, the Interdoc network has been at the forefront of development in the non-commercial sector's use of e-mail. For many users in NGOs, Interdoc — along with its other functions — is perceived as a network of NGOs using e-mail. It has an international membership with many member organisations based in the South. The network itself remains rather a nebulous affair. It has not really developed a strong identity beyond the sum of the active participants. This is very much in the spirit of the original founders who were above all concerned that Interdoc should be an informal network which does not develop a 'life' of its own. The success of Interdoc, the spread of information technology and the spread of e-mail may, however, eventually force the network to adopt a more formal structure.

In practice much of the work of Interdoc has focused on the sharing of technical knowledge. A Technical Advisory Group was appointed in 1987 and this body, together with the secretariat and the Steering Group members, has dealt with numerous enquiries. One of the most successful features of the work of the network has been the involvement of Interdoc members in a wide range of conferences and workshops concerning information technology and e-mail. At these meetings Interdoc has sought to maintain a balanced, open exchange between NGOs and technicians. At least 15 major events have been organised in developing countries since the network was formed. Many of these have proved to be unusually productive and stimulating, and have helped to facilitate further initiatives both within and outside of the Interdoc network.

In May 1990 Interdoc organised a major conference 'Information Exchange for Social Change' in the Netherlands. This event brought together a truly worldwide cross-section of information users, information providers and information carriers. It was particularly notable as a forum in which NGOs, campaigning organisations, resource workers and researchers could meet and exchange views with technical consultants and the e-mail system operators.

E-mail: E-mail was identified as a pilot project for investigation when Interdoc was founded. It rapidly became a dominant theme in the work of the network. Interdoc is involved in a number of bulletin boards on different e-mail systems. The main Interdoc-BBS bulletin board on the GeoNet system is an important forum for the exchange of all kinds of information.

In keeping with the pioneering spirit of the network, Interdoc members are closely involved in the development of NGO databases, including the Nigel database on the Poptel/GeoNet and APC systems. It is envisaged that such databases will, in the future, play an important role in the exchange of information between NGOs, avoiding some of the shortcomings currently associated with bulletin boards. Interdoc members are also involved in experiments with inexpensive alternatives to packet switching (see Chapter 7), such as the Fidonet bulletin board system and the transfer of data by radio.

People's Access

People's Access is a non-profit-making body offering advice, support and training on all aspects of computing to people's organisations in the Philippines. It was formed in 1987 following a meeting between several NGOs in the Philippines. Membership of People's Access is open to people's organisations and people's service institutions. By the beginning of 1990 there were 22 such members. Organisations that do not fall under these categories, and individuals, may join People's Access as 'special members'. The organisation offers regular training courses on a wide variety of topics including basic computing, word processing, database management, spreadsheet applications, desktop publishing, computer communications and computerised bookkeeping.

People's Access uses 50 per cent of its membership subscriptions to cover the cost of manuals, magazines and books for members' use. It reprints a selection of useful articles for members and produces a regular newsletter. In addition to training and library facilities, People's Access offers consultancy on all aspects of information handling, including systems analysis and the evaluation of computer hardware needs. People's Access also offers hardware maintenance to members.

E-Mail: An important aspect of the work of People's Access is the provision of a local bulletin board called ACCESS-BBS. This bulletin board — or small e-mail system — is operated primarily for the benefit of members of People's Access. There are, however, some areas of the bulletin board that are open to non-members. This enables outsiders to contribute to the ongoing debates and discussions. Around 11 member organisations, 25 non-member organisations and 200 individuals use the system.

People's Access maintains a daily gateway from the ACCESS system to the international GeoNet e-mail system. It is possible for users of other e-mail systems to swap messages with any users of the local ACCESS system. The nature of this traffic covers the whole spectrum from personal travel arrangements to the circulation of project proposals between funders and their partners. People's Access regularly posts news summaries provided by members on relevant GeoNet bulletin boards.

In 1988, People's Access was involved in a three-month experimental project using the Fidonet bulletin board and communications system to link up with participants in Hong Kong, Indonesia, Thailand and Malaysia. A valuable lesson which People's Access drew from this experience was that the use of Fidonet for international link-ups will not flourish unless there are already active local bulletin boards in existence. Based on its South East Asian and local experience, the present thrust of the work of People's Access is, therefore, to encourage the setting-up and use of local bulletin board services, whether public, private, commercial or service-orientated. The ACCESS bulletin board and e-mail system is intended mainly to facilitate information exchange between other people's organisations and networks.

Fax and telex machines are extremely expensive in the Philippines so the transmission of fax and telex messages via e-mail is an important alternative for many organisations. The major problem experienced by People's Access with regard to the use of e-mail is an unreliable telephone service and noisy telephone lines.

Satis

Member organisations of the Satis network aim to apply technology in the service of sustainable development, and to add value to the resources of the poor. They are involved in fields such as health, agriculture, habitat, water supply, sanitation, energy and transport. The aim of this work is to help local community enterprises 'to raise living standards, raise issues, raise funds, raise income and to raise — and meet — expectations'. The network is made up of almost 100 member organisations in over 50 countries. It produces a range of resource materials including the Satis Catalog. This is a comprehensive list of over 1,600 books, manuals and audio-visuals available from Satis member organisations around the world. It is also developing the Satis Information System. This is a widely-used system, tailored particularly to the needs of small information centres, dealing with practical development and environmental issues. The development of this standardised information system greatly improves the possibilities for information exchange between different centres. To a degree, the work of Satis in this field is similar to the work of Huridocs in the field of human rights documentation (see page 44). The Information System includes the Satis Classification, standard formats and a thesaurus. These tools aim to provide a comprehensive system for the registration, retrieval and exchange of information on technology, environment and sustainable development. A software package, called SatisFile, is under preparation.

Satis also administers a system of 'Satis Tokens', which provide an international 'currency' for clients wanting to purchase services from Satis members, but who face problems in obtaining or transferring hard currency. In addition to its 'traditional' services in information science and communication, Satis has expanded into the field of technology marketing and replication. It supports member organisations in the marketing and dissemination of their 'success stories'. Recent examples have included oilseed technology, wheelchair production, bicycle manufacture, water pumping and mushroom cultivation.

E-mail: 'Electronic mail is essential to Satis' states a Satis publication. 'We want a daily work-style that reflects our philosophy of decentralisation, speed, equal access for all partners, at high cost benefit'. Satis administers its own account, known as Satisnet, on the GeoNet system that is made up of several dozen mailboxes. It is used for the exchange of technical information, document transfer, co-publishing and communication with the secretariat.

Satis runs a public bulletin board called Satisfaction on the GeoNet system. The network has also been involved in the development of an NGO database on the Poptel/GeoNet system. The Satis Catalog of materials available from member organisations has been available in the database since the introduction of the pilot project.

Staff of the small secretariat use e-mail to carry on their work when travelling away from the office. There are plans to move the secretariat from the Netherlands to a Third World location and to create regional secretariats worldwide. E-mail will, therefore, play an increasingly important role in the internal administrative work of the network.

PART TWO
TECHNICAL

PART TWO: TECHNICAL

Chapters 4-7

It is possible to use e-mail without knowing all the technical details. The knowledge of many e-mail users does not extend beyond knowing 'which button to push'. Organisations that run small e-mail systems generally offer excellent technical support to both new and established users. Most are prepared to offer help over the telephone and can provide formal training, some also sell hardware and software that is pre-configured to work with their particular system. In addition, the e-mail system may well be able to provide a list of contacts and volunteers who can help with the installation and use of e-mail.

The technical detail provided here is intended as a supplement to these other sources of information. It will help organisations to become more self-sufficient in their use of e-mail since, without some understanding of the operation of the system, the slightest change or alteration will cause problems that require outside help. Understanding the principles of e-mail will also help users to develop and make full use of the system that is available to them.

Part Two begins with a section explaining a few unavoidable jargon terms that appear frequently in the following text. Chapter 4 covers hardware and software — the equipment (including the modem) needed to participate in an e-mail network. Chapter 5 looks at the theory behind data transmission. It explains how the modem and computer must be set up to communicate with an e-mail network. Chapter 6 examines the methods whereby data is actually transmitted between the microcomputer and the e-mail host computer. It looks at *ASCII* text file transfer, file transfer protocols and error correction techniques. Chapter 7 concentrates on the telephone network and packet switching.

Unavoidable jargon; bits, bytes, ASCII, text files and binary files

This brief section introduces some computer jargon that it has simply not been possible to avoid in the coming pages. The terms in question are: bits, bytes, ASCII, text files and binary files.

The smallest unit of information stored by a computer is a bit. Bit stands for Binary digIT. Binary refers to a counting system that only uses 1s and 0s. 01001101 is an example of a number in the binary counting system. This number is equivalent to 77 in our normal decimal counting system. Each digit in a binary number can only be a 1 or a 0. The number 01001101 is made up of 8 binary digits or bits. The binary counting system is used in computing because it relates to the internal workings of a computer. A computer is made up of millions of electrical components. These components can only be 'on' or 'off'. To illuminate this point one might imagine an ordinary house light switch which can only be on or off (or broken). There is no in-between state of 'half on' or 'half off'. Binary counting can be used to represent the state of these electrical components within a computer. A binary 1 represents 'on' while a binary 0 represents 'off'. When data is transmitted between two computers using modems — between a personal computer and the central host computer of an e-mail system, for example — it is transmitted one bit at a time. A series of signals representing binary 1s and 0s — the bits — is sent down the telephone line.

As mentioned, the bit is the smallest unit of information stored by a computer. A bit can only have a value of 1 or 0. In microcomputers, bits are stored together in groups of 8 bits called a byte. A byte is the unit that stores one character of information (in text files at least). Such a character could be a letter of the alphabet, a number between 0 and 9, or a punctuation mark. Bits are the building blocks of bytes. Bytes are the building blocks of text files and other computer data files. The binary number given above — 01001101 — could represent a byte. Any particular byte (ie 8 bits) can have 256 different values ranging from 00000000 to 11111111 (the decimal numbers 0 to 255).

The American Standard Code for Information Interchange (ASCII) is a widely accepted standard for microcomputers which assigns the different values of a byte to represent different characters. ASCII is a kind of 'alphabet' for microcomputers. The number 01001101 represents the letter 'M' in the ASCII standard, while lower case 'm' is represented by 01101101. The transmission of computer text data as strings of binary numbers representing ASCII codes is similar in principle to the

55

transmission of text using the old Morse code system. The 1s and 0s of binary numbers correspond to the dots and dashes of Morse code.

The ASCII standard is not entirely universal since there exists some degree of regional variation. British ASCII, for example, departs from the US original by assigning the decimal number 35 to represent the pound sterling sign (£) rather than the hash sign (#). In general, however, there are only minor variations in the ASCII standard between numbers 0 and 127. The first 32 are reserved for special control characters used by the computer and printer. The rest are used for all the letters, numbers and symbols (!, ? etc) that are found on a normal microcomputer keyboard.

A text file consists entirely of bytes representing text characters. It does not contain any of the special ASCII control codes, except the code for carriage return and a special code marking the end of the file. The fact that all microcomputers use the ASCII standard greatly enhances the possibilities for information interchange between different computers and different software packages. The transmission of plain ASCII text files is one of the cornerstones of international e-mail since most potential problems of incompatibility are avoided in this way.

Some computer files, however, are not text files. The ASCII standard does not apply for these files. An example of a non-text file is a spreadsheet data file. Spreadsheet packages, such as Lotus 123, are used to store and manipulate financial data. A spreadsheet is rather like a word processor for numbers. It can carry out complex calculations and analyses. The spreadsheet data stored on disc is not held as text, so it cannot be stored in ASCII code. Instead it is held as a series of binary numbers. For this reason a spreadsheet data file is referred to as a binary file. Another common example of a binary file is a computer program. Again, this is not a text file but rather a string of binary commands for the computer. E-mail systems handle binary files differently from ASCII text files. Normally e-mail users swap ASCII text messages. Special procedures are necessary to transmit binary files.

Hardware and software 4

The computer

In theory it is possible to use most types of personal computer to send and receive e-mail. Subscribers do not need to have 'compatible' machines to swap mail since all messages are sent via the central host computer.

Throughout the world the most common type of personal computer is the 'PC'. This is either a genuine IBM PC or a copy of the original machine made by one of a myriad of smaller companies. IBM is the largest computer manufacturer in the world. An e-mail member can, however, equally well use a microcomputer that is not compatible with the IBM PC. The Apple Mac and the Atari ST are two common examples. Then there are the cheapest, 'bottom end' computers which are neither compatible with the standard IBM PC nor with each other. In theory, there is no reason why such computers cannot be used for e-mail. The limiting factor is whether an acceptable communications software package (see page 68) is available for the computer in question. In other words, whether any programs have been written for a particular model that will let it be used for e-mail without too much fuss. The Amstrad PCW is an example of a cheap, non-PC compatible computer. It can be used for e-mail with a special communications program called Chit Chat.

There remains one small jargon term to be explained: expansion slots. These are, quite literally, free slots located inside most PC-style computers. Expansion cards can be fitted into the free expansion slots. These are cards — about the height of a postcard but longer — that carry electronic circuitry and chips. Expansion cards are used to enhance the performance of the computer in areas desired by the user. It is, for example, possible to fit a 'graphics'

57

card that will improve the screen display of a standard PC-type computer. It is normally fairly simple to fit an expansion card although it will be necessary to take the casing off the computer. Small, portable computers may not have any expansion slots. Expansion cards may be used to fit an internal modem or a serial port to a computer. These possibilities are described in greater detail on pages 60 and 67.

The modem

Modem stands for 'MOdulator — DEModulator'. A modem is, at the present time, always required when sending or reading e-mail. Modulation in this context means that information held by the computer as bits and bytes is translated into a form that can be transmitted over ordinary, voice telephone lines. Demodulation refers to the converse process of converting incoming signals into a form that a computer can interpret.

A computer holds information in the form of bytes made up of bits. Each bit is a distinct entity. Information is sent from the computer as a string of 1s and 0s. This is known as 'digital transmission'. A telephone line, on the other hand, carries sounds in 'wave' form. Any value (within certain limits) is possible on a line, not just 1s and 0s. This is known as 'analogue' transmission.

All but the most modern telephone systems were designed in order to carry ordinary voice conversations. They developed before it was necessary to pay any regard to the needs of computer data transmissions. A modem is necessary only because older analogue telephone systems cannot directly carry digital computer data transmissions. The modem is simply a box which sits between the computer and the telephone system converting one kind of information flow into another: digital computer data into analogue telephone signals and vice versa. Slow speed modems will, in effect, simply translate binary 1s and 0s into different tones to be sent across the telephone network. The telephone networks of the future will also be digital rather than analogue networks. They will be designed with regard to both voice and data transmission. These digital telephone networks will be able to

58

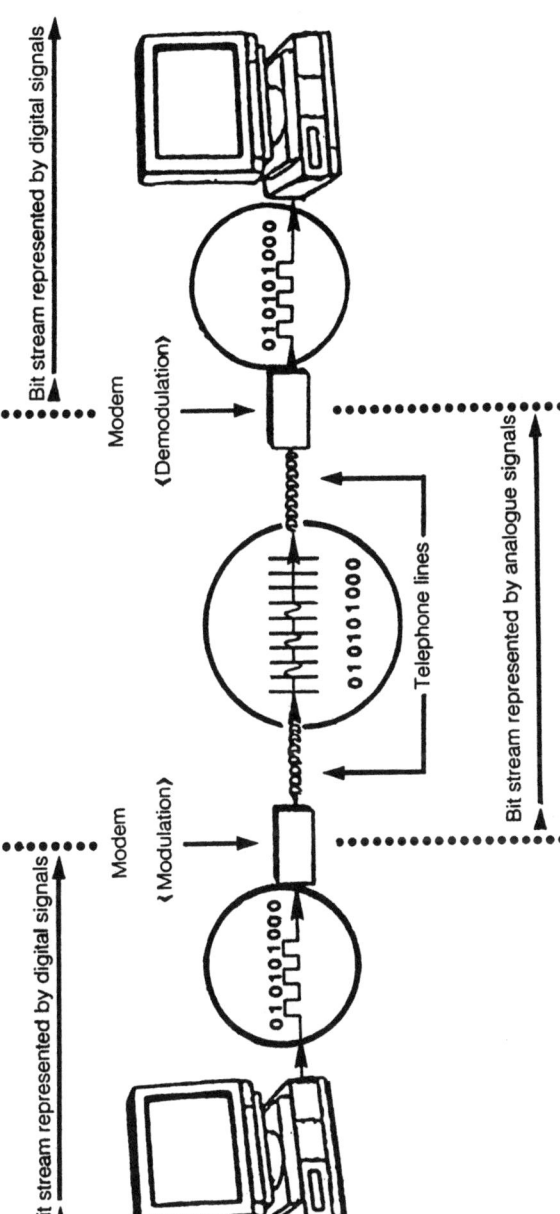

Figure 3: *Microcomputer and modem* A modem is currently always required when data is transmitted over a telephone system. The modem transforms the digital data held by a computer into an analogue wave form which can be transmitted over a normal telephone line, and vice versa.

carry data transmissions directly. It will be possible to send data on these networks without using a modem. Development is under way to introduce digital networks in major cities in most developed countries.

There are two different types of modem: internal and external. A normal external modem is a small box about the size of an average hardback book. The modem is connected to the computer by a serial cable (see page 67). A second cable from the modem plugs directly into a standard telephone socket. It is also possible to buy small external modems, known as pocket modems, that are about the size of a packet of cigarettes. Most pocket modems can screw straight on to the serial socket of a computer instead of using a serial cable and run off normal mains power or from an internal battery. They are often used in conjunction with portable computers.

External modems often have a series of little indicator lights on the front panel. These will light up or flicker to show what the modem is doing at any given time. They can provide useful clues about possible problems if the system is not working properly.

An internal modem is a card carrying various circuitry and chips. The card fits into an expansion slot inside the personal computer. All modern PC compatible computers have some internal expansion slots. A computer fitted with an internal modem will have a telephone cable coming from the modem out of the back of the computer. This telephone cable plugs directly into a telephone socket. Both external and internal modems may be fitted with a little speaker that allows the user to hear what is happening on the line. Like the indicator lights on an external modem, this can be useful for trouble-shooting.

There is generally little to choose between internal and external modems. External modems may be more convenient. They may have the little indicator lights for diagnostics, they are easier to install and can more easily be moved between different computers. On the negative side, they require that the microcomputer is fitted with a serial port (see page 66). A point in favour of internal modems is that they are generally a little cheaper than external modems.

In most developed countries modems can be purchased in the same way as other computer equipment. In some developing countries, however, one is obliged to rent or buy modems from the local telecommunications company. In other countries there is a large fee for registering a modem with the authorities.

Acoustic coupler

The attentive reader will, no doubt, be wondering what can be done in situations where the telephone is directly wired into the telephone network. Telephones in hotels, for example, are seldom connected by a plug to a telephone socket. Instead they are connected directly to a junction box. This is done to discourage the guests from taking the phone set with them when they leave. Telephone sockets are also rare in some developing countries which have old telephone networks. How can a modem be 'plugged' into the telephone network?

In these situations there are at least three possible solutions. Firstly, in many developing countries, it may be possible to find someone who — either officially or unofficially — will fit a telephone socket. A more dramatic alternative is to take the cover off the telephone junction box and use a telephone wire fitted with 'crocodile clips' to attach the modem directly onto the exposed telephone wires. A third option is to use a special kind of modem called an acoustic coupler. An acoustic coupler consists of a modem fitted with two rubber cups. The telephone hand set slots into these cups and transmission proceeds as normal. Acoustic couplers are 'old' technology. They are notorious for introducing interference or line noise into transmissions and should be avoided unless there is no alternative.

Hayes compatibility

Modems will often boast of being Hayes compatible. Hayes is an American modem manufacturer. The company developed a special set of commands that is used to control the workings of a modem. This command set became so widespread that today it is a de facto standard. Other manufacturers now produce modems that respond to the same set of commands as Hayes modems.

All Hayes commands begin with the letters AT, which stand for ATtention. These must be in capitals. When a Hayes compatible modem receives the characters AT from a

61

microcomputer it prepares to accept a command directed to the modem. The command to dial a number in the Hayes command set is D followed by the telephone number. Thus, if a computer sends to a Hayes compatible modem the message ATD8405500, then the modem will automatically dial the number 8405500. The command ATZ will cancel all previous instructions and return the modem to its original settings. This is like 're-booting' (re-starting) a computer — useful if you get completely stuck.

A communications software program is necessary in order to transmit data from a microcomputer. 'Comms' packages are described on page 68. Such communications packages for microcomputers are invariably written to work with Hayes compatible modems. This means that they will work with any normal modem that supports the Hayes command set, regardless of manufacturer. Many communications software packages can also be used to drive non-Hayes compatible modems. To do this, however, will be a little more complicated and will require a degree of technical understanding.

Modem speeds

All modems work at certain pre-defined speeds. The different speeds for modems are defined by international standards. Different models of modem will offer different possible speeds of operation. The higher the speed, the higher the price of the modem. A cheap modem, for example, might only offer one slow speed. A more expensive modem might offer a high speed and additional slower speeds. When running at a high speed the computer and modem transmit more characters per second. The connect time to the e-mail system — and consequently the charges — are thereby reduced.

It is essential that the sending modem and the receiving modem should operate at the same speed. This is why a fast, expensive modem will also offer lower speeds — it may have to link up with slower modems. In addition, transmission at slower speeds is less susceptible to interference. It may be desirable to drop down to a lower speed on a noisy line.

The most common transmission speeds for modems used with personal computers are 300 bits per second (bps), 1200 bps and

2400 bps. There is also a hybrid option for 'split speed' transmission at 1200/75 bits per second. This means that the modem transmits at only 75 bps but can receive at speeds of up to 1200 bps. Split speed operation requires a little explanation. It derives from the world of computer terminals where information is retrieved from a database on a large, central mainframe computer. In this situation a user will type in short queries at the keyboard ('find such and such'), and the mainframe will conduct a search and transmit the relevant information back to the terminal. The user only transmits small amounts of slow speed data (the queries) while the mainframe returns large volumes of high speed data (the replies). As a consequence, modems with a slow sending speed but a fast receiving speed may be used. These are cheaper than modems that can both send and receive at a higher speed such as 1200 bps. Modems offering split speed transmission at 1200/75 bps will invariably also have an option for transmission and reception at 300 bps. There is no reason why such modems cannot be used for e-mail. The 300 bps option is used for sending mail (this is faster than sending at the alternative speed of 75 bps). The 1200 bps option is used for reading mail (since receiving at 1200 bps is faster than receiving at the alternative speed of 300 bps). The chief drawback of this system is that you have to place two calls — one to read mail and one to send mail. This is clearly a bit odd. It results from the fact that the modem is being used for a task other than that for which it was developed.

In recent years the prices of modems have dropped to a point where it is worth going straight for a 1200/1200 bps modem and avoiding split speed operation all together. Any 1200/1200 bps modem should also have an option for slower transmission at 300/300 bps since this is more robust on poor lines. Many agencies in developed countries are, in fact, purchasing high-speed 2400 bps modems (which also offer transmission at 1200 and 300 bps). In general terms transmission speeds will continue to rise, so high-speed modems represent an investment for the future.

Modem standards

As mentioned, there are international standards that define the speeds of operation for modems. These standards also define the

63

technical details of how the computer data is converted into signals that can be carried on telephone lines designed for voices. Unfortunately, there are two sets of standards which are not entirely compatible. All European countries use a set of standards evolved by a body called CCITT. The USA uses the so-called Bell standards. Developing countries might use either standard. In Central and Latin America, however, the Bell standards have been universally adopted. In general the different standards are not too much of a problem for e-mail users, who will normally only be dialling the local packet switching exchange (see Chapter 7). The important point in this case is simply to make sure that the correct type of modem is purchased initially. Other types of data transfer, such as direct connections between two personal computers, may be more tricky as a result of the differing modem standards.

CCITT and Bell standards define the same transmission speeds but they differ in the technicalities of how the data is transmitted on the phone line. Thus, for example, the CCITT standard called 'V21' and the Bell standard called '103/113' both operate at 300 bits per second but they are not compatible.

The CCITT standards for data transmission over telephone lines are known as the 'V' series recommendations. Many of these V series recommendations relate to high speed modems used on private lines. Such modems are not normally used for e-mail. The summary of CCITT and Bell standards opposite only covers those that might be used for e-mail in non-commercial organisations.

In recent years, American modem manufacturers have tended to comply with new CCITT standards. V22bis (2400 bps), for example, is found on US modems. It is possible to buy modems that can operate according to both Bell and CCITT V series standards.

There is also a CCITT standard, V32, for modems operating at 9600 bits per second. Modems offering this standard are, at present, still too expensive for most NGOs. In addition, this standard is not widely offered by e-mail systems or other services. It may, however, become more widespread amongst non-commercial users in the future.

CCITT standards

V21	Send and receive at 300 bits per second. Not compatible with Bell 103/113 which is the equivalent US standard.
V22	Send and receive at speeds up to 1200 bits per second. Theoretically compatible with Bell 212A which is the equivalent US standard.
V22bis	Send and receive at speeds up to 2400 bits per second.
V23	Split speed operation. Send at 75 bits per second, receive at 1200 bits per second.

Bell standards

103/113	Send and receive at 300 bits per second. Not compatible with V21 which is the equivalent CCITT standard.
212A	Send and receive at 1200 bits per second. Theoretically compatible with V22 which is the equivalent CCITT standard.

Serial interfaces

In computer jargon 'peripherals' are pieces of equipment which can be attached to the actual computer. Modems and printers are both peripherals. There are two different ways in which information can flow between a computer and a peripheral — through a serial interface or through a parallel interface. Interface, in this context, means the same as connection — it refers to the actual link-up between the computer and the peripheral.

To link a computer and a peripheral through a serial interface

65

it is necessary that the computer and the peripheral are both fitted with similar serial sockets and that there is a special serial cable to plug between them. The sockets are called ports in computer jargon. Similarly, a parallel interface between a computer and a peripheral requires that the computer and the peripheral are both fitted with parallel ports (sockets) and that there is a suitable parallel cable to plug between them.

A printer is normally linked to a personal computer through a parallel interface but it is also possible to link it through a serial interface. Most printers are supplied with a parallel port as standard while the serial port is an optional extra that must be bought and fitted separately. A modem is always linked to a computer through a serial interface.

The principle of serial transmission is that the smallest units of data, bits, are sent one after another in a single stream down a single wire. In parallel transmission, by contrast, a group of eight bits, called a byte, is sent simultaneously down eight separate wires. Each type of transmission has advantages and disadvantages.

Besides the wires that actually carry the data, there will be other wires carrying messages that regulate the flow of data. The computer and the peripheral will exchange signals indicating that they are ready to send data, ready to receive data, requesting a pause in the transmission and so forth. These messages are not part of the actual information being transmitted, they are used to control the flow of data. For this reason a serial interface between a computer and a peripheral might actually consist of nine separate wires in one cable. Only two of these wires are actually used to carry the data — one to transmit and one to receive — while others may be used to control the flow of the data.

RS-232C or V24

The discussion has so far been on a theoretical level. In practice serial interfaces come in various shapes and sizes. A 'standard', in this context, means that somebody has defined what each wire in a cable will do, what physical shape the ports (sockets) will have, how many pins they will have and so forth.

RS-232C is one such standard. It defines the form of serial interface that is most commonly used in PC-type personal computers. The RS-232C serial interface is defined by an American standards body. The same serial interface is also called V24 by CCITT, the international standards body. Most commonly, however, the interface is simply referred to as RS-232. An RS-232 port is 'D' shaped with either nine or 25 pins in two rows. In both the nine pin and the 25 pin version only a few of the pins are used. The rest are redundant. Personal computers, especially PCs, are invariably fitted with a parallel printer port as a standard feature. Most will also come with an RS-232 serial port as standard. In some cheaper models, however, the serial port will be an optional extra which must be purchased and fitted separately. This potential cost should not be overlooked when calculating the costs of installing e-mail.

The RS-232 port fitted to a computer may either be the nine pin or the 25 pin variety. Small nine pin to 25 pin adaptor cables are easily obtainable, if required. The RS-232 25 pin port is actually the same shape as the normal parallel port found on the back of PC-type personal computers. The parallel port will probably be labelled 'printer' while the serial port, if fitted, may be labelled 'serial','RS-232' or 'modem'. The parallel port on a PC-style computer will be 'female' while the serial port on a computer will be 'male'. An external modem will always have an RS-232 port fitted as standard. The serial port on the modem will be female.

Unfortunately, the RS-232 specification is not strictly adhered to and there are numerous variations between RS-232 ports from different manufacturers. This can cause many practical problems when dealing with RS-232 interfaces.

RS-232 cables

An RS-232 modem cable in needed to link the modem to the computer. A serial modem cable will be female at one end and male at the other. An RS-232 printer cable, used to link a computer to a printer, is normally also male at one end and female at the other. However, despite the fact that a serial modem cable and a serial printer cable look identical they are in fact different and cannot be used interchangeably.

In a standard RS-232 port found on a computer or a printer, pin 2 is used to send data and pin 3 is used to receive data. In a serial printer cable the wires attached to pins 2 and 3 are 'crossed over'. In other words, the wire attached to pin 2 at one end is attached to pin 3 at the other end and vice versa. A message sent by the computer out of pin 2 (used to transmit data). will be received by the printer using pin 3 (which receives data). And vice versa. Two wires that control the flow of the data will also be 'crossed'. In a modem cable, by contrast, there is a 'one to one' connection. The wire attached to pin 2 at one end is also attached to pin 2 at the other end and likewise for pin 3. A standard RS-232 serial port for a modem is, in fact, slightly different from the RS-232 port on a printer or computer. It is designed to send and receive data from a computer without any need to 'cross over' the send and receive wires in the cable.

A third variety of RS-232 cable is a 'null modem' cable. This is typically used to link together two adjacent computers. As in the case of a serial printer cable, the send and receive wires (pins 2 and 3) are 'crossed over'. Unlike a printer cable, however, both ends of a null modem cable will generally be female.

In summary, there are different types of RS-232 serial cable that are not interchangeable. It is advisable for new e-mail users to make sure that they get the correct modem cable when getting the modem.

None of the above applies if an internal modem is used. An internal modem will fit directly into an expansion slot inside the computer. There is a direct connection between the computer and the modem, so an RS-232 interface is not needed. For this reason an internal modem may be preferable in the case of a computer that does not have a serial port fitted as a standard feature.

Communications software

In order to use e-mail, it is necessary to run a communications program on the personal computer, just as it is necessary to 'load' and 'run' a word processing package before a computer can be used for word processing. There is a wide variety of communications software programs — or comms packages — on the market.

The function of the communications software is to regulate the flow of information into and out of the computer. If, for example, the flow of information from the central host to the personal computer is too fast for the PC, then the communications package will send a message requesting that the e-mail host should pause until the PC has processed the backlog of incoming information. The communications package will also regulate the process of sending files directly from disc and of capturing incoming text directly on to disc.

In addition, the communications package will offer various file transfer protocols. These allow files other than ASCII text files to be transmitted. A non-text file might be a formatted document held as a word processor file or financial information stored in a 'spreadsheet'. There is more on the subject of file transfer protocols in Chapter 6. At this point it is sufficient to say that any decent communications package should offer at least two file transfer protocols: X-modem and Kermit.

Besides these basic functions, the communications software will offer a variety of features designed to make life easier for e-mail users, including some simple method for altering the settings of the modem and the computer. (There is more about these settings, known as modem or line settings, in Chapter 5.) It should also offer a facility to store frequently used telephone numbers together with their associated computer and modem settings. When a number is selected, the communications software should be capable of automatically preparing the computer and modem for transmission and then dialling the number. Another useful feature offered by most communications packages is the possibility of creating 'macros'. In order to connect up to the packet switching and e-mail systems, it is necessary to go through a log on procedure which involves typing complicated identification codes of various kinds. The log on procedure is exactly the same every time. It can become extremely tedious if you are calling the e-mail system once or twice a day. Keyboard macros 'record' a sequence of keys typed at the keyboard — for example the log on procedure. One touch of a key will 'replay' these key strokes and thereby automatically transmit the log on sequence. Macros can go a long way towards making e-mail usage simple and painless.

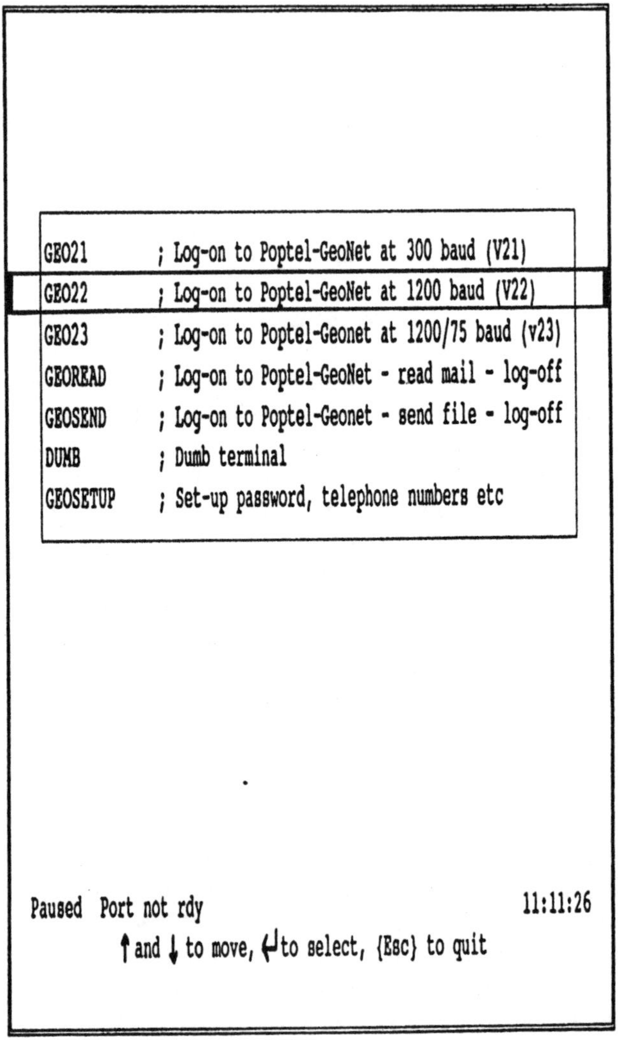

```
GEO21        ; Log-on to Poptel-GeoNet at 300 baud (V21)
GEO22        ; Log-on to Poptel-GeoNet at 1200 baud (V22)
GEO23        ; Log-on to Poptel-Geonet at 1200/75 baud (v23)
GEOREAD      ; Log-on to Poptel-GeoNet - read mail - log-off
GEOSEND      ; Log-on to Poptel-Geonet - send file - log-off
DUMB         ; Dumb terminal
GEOSETUP     ; Set-up password, telephone numbers etc
```

```
Paused  Port not rdy                              11:11:26
        ↑ and ↓ to move, ↵ to select, {Esc} to quit
```

Figure 4: *Poptalk communications package* The Poptalk
package is written specifically to work with the Poptel/GeoNet
e-mail system. The logon procedure is fully automated. A user
needs only to highlight an option with the cursor bar and press
return. The GEOREAD and GEOSEND options automatically
read or send mail.

HARDWARE AND SOFTWARE

Popular communications packages: Procomm, Mirror II and Poptalk

Of the numerous communications packages on sale, Procomm is one of the most widespread in NGO and hobbyist circles. Procomm is a good package. It offers all the features mentioned above, is straightforward to use and makes funny little noises like an arcade game. These sound effects are guaranteed to impress onlookers, but can be switched off if necessary. Procomm's success is due in part to the fact that it was introduced as a 'shareware' package. Unlike other commercial packages, it is permissible to copy Procomm with the aim of trying it out. Anyone who regularly uses the package is then required to send a small registration fee to the authors at an address given on the disc. Procomm costs a fraction of the price of many similar commercially distributed packages. There is now a successor to Procomm called Procomm Plus. Unlike its forebear, Procomm Plus is not a shareware package but it is still very good value. It has several enhanced features such as improved keyboard macros.

Another common package is Mirror II. This program was, for a while, 'bundled' (thrown in) with a portable computer made by Amstrad. The computer is itself supplied with an internal, high-speed modem. The whole offer was quite popular with 'budget-conscious' individuals and small organisations using e-mail, and aided the spread of Mirror. Mirror II is a versatile and powerful package but an inexperienced user will not find it particularly easy to master. It is not very 'user friendly' although there are facilities to automate much of the operation using Mirror macros. The Mirror package is governed by the normal rules for commercial software which do not permit copies of the program to be made, except for backups. In relation to some other communications packages, Mirror is quite expensive. There is also a new version available — Mirror III. Among the additional features of Mirror III are improved error correction techniques, including MNP (see page 96).

Poptalk is an interesting communications package. It is written by the co-operative that runs a host computer of the GeoNet e-mail system and specialises in providing services for non-commercial users. The Poptalk package is written specifically to work with the GeoNet e-mail system. It will not currently work

71

with any other system. For users of the GeoNet system, however, it is extremely simple to use. All the relevant settings for the modem, password etc are entered just once when the program is first 'installed'. The e-mail co-op will normally be able to help with this initial process. When the program is correctly installed it is possible, quite literally, to read the e-mail at the touch of a single button. The opening menu offers a number of options to log on to the system at various speeds. Highlighting one of these options with the cursor bar and pressing the return key will take the user straight into GeoNet. The GEOREAD option from the main Poptalk menu will automatically log on to GeoNet, read all new messages, capture them to disc on the personal computer and log off again, returning the user to the opening menu. The whole process for logging on and off should take less than a minute while the time taken to read new messages will depend on their length and number. In similar fashion, a specified file can automatically be sent to a specified user by selecting the GEOSEND option. It can often be complicated and confusing for inexperienced users to come to grips with e-mail. The Poptalk program is an imaginative and successful attempt to tackle this problem. It swaps flexibility and power for a package which is extremely easy to use.

Data communications 5

This chapter concentrates on the actual transmission of data from one computer to another. It has already been noted that a computer is always linked to a modem by a serial interface, transmitting a single stream of individual bits. By contrast, a parallel interface (frequently used to connect a computer to a printer) carries one byte consisting of eight bits (ie one character) simultaneously down eight separate wires.

In the case of e-mail, the microcomputer and the e-mail host computer exchange data in serial fashion via modems. The sending computer breaks each byte to be transmitted into a stream of bits. These are sent down the telephone line and then reconstructed into bytes by the receiving computer.

The question arises, how is the receiving computer able to 'interpret' the string of incoming bits in such a way that the original bytes are correctly reconstructed? The answer is that the sending and the receiving computer must be set up so that they both handle the data transmission in a similar fashion.

After briefly explaining the concept of asynchronous data communications, the remainder of this chapter examines the variables that can affect the transmission of data between two computers. These include the settings governing the actual serial data transfer (referred to as the 'line settings'), the speed of transmission, and the local software settings.

Synchronous and asynchronous data communication

Personal computers transmit data in asynchronous mode (the terms will be explained shortly). Larger mainframe computer systems may use a different form of data transfer known as 'synchronous' transmission. Except for this brief explanation of the terms, the rest of this chapter deals only with asynchronous communications since synchronous transmission is not relevant to e-mail using personal computers. In the case of synchronous data transfer, the sender and recipient are 'synchronised'. This is achieved through special timing codes transmitted at the beginning of each session. Data is then transmitted in a steady stream at pre-determined intervals. The recipient always knows exactly when to expect the next bit.

Asynchronous communication — sometimes referred to as start/stop mode — does not require the sender and recipient to be synchronised. The sending computer first sends a bit — called the start bit — which signals 'I-am-going-to-send-some-data'. It then transmits a pre-determined number of bits of actual data. These data bits normally represent one byte — in other words, one character. A parity bit (see page 76) may follow the data bits. Finally, one or more stop bits are transmitted signalling 'now-I-have-finished-sending-data'. Then the whole process starts again with the next start bit. In asynchronous mode the transmission of each byte of data is, in effect, a separate event. Each unit of information consists of a number of data bits surrounded by framing bits (the start and stop bits). The framing bits are necessary to ensure that the two computers 'understand' one another.

Synchronous communication is more efficient than asynchronous communication because more time is spent sending data bits and less time is spent sending framing bits. Synchronous data transmission over a telephone line requires a special modem and special communications software. Modems capable of synchronous transmission are more expensive and sophisticated than asynchronous modems but they are also more efficient.

Line settings

The line setting defines a number of different variables so that one computer can correctly re-assemble bytes of data from the stream of bits transmitted by the sending computer.

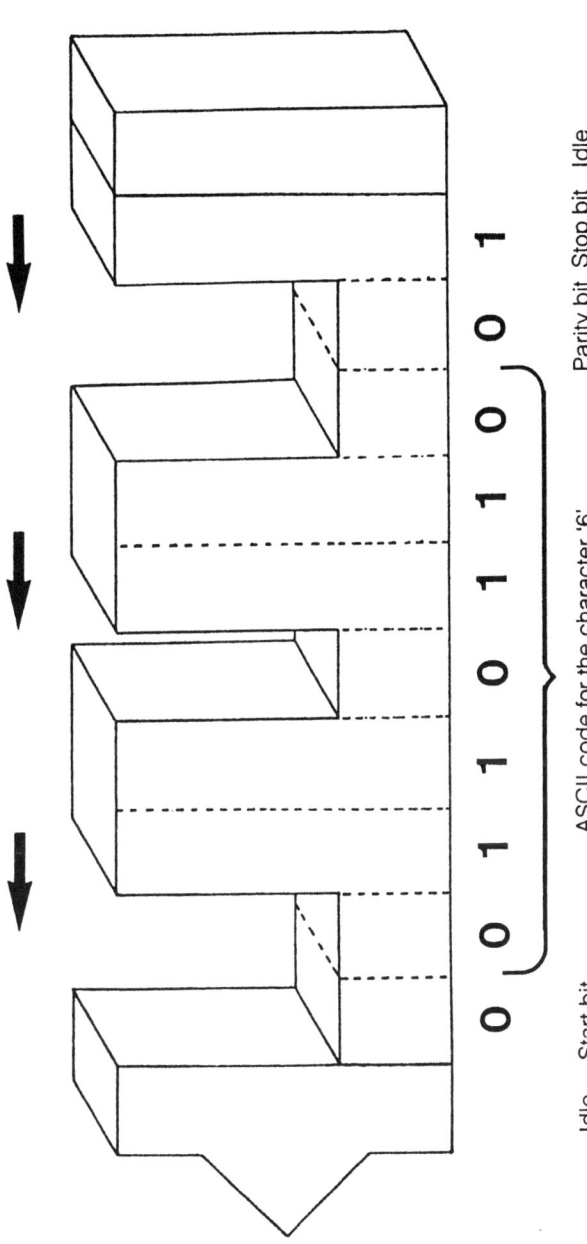

0	0	0	1	1	0	1	1	0	0	1	1
Idle	Start bit		ASCII code for the character '6'						Parity bit	Stop bit	Idle

Figure 5: Asynchronous data transmission In asynchronous transmission each character, represented by the data bits, is framed by a start bit, stop bit and, possibly, a parity bit.

PART TWO: TECHNICAL

In the case of an e-mail network the line settings used by the central host computer will be decided by the people who run the e-mail system. They will provide new members with information about the line settings to be used. It is then up to the user to set up his or her personal computer so that it uses the same line settings. If the new member uses the wrong line settings then they will probably not be able to establish contact with the central host. If they do manage to get a connection then the screen may fill up with strings of garbage rather than recognisable text. No damage will be done but it may take a bit of experimentation to find the right settings. Problems with line settings are one of the most common difficulties experienced by new users.

This section will examine each of the variables in the line setting. These are: data bits, stop bits, parity bit and transmission speed. The start bit is not included in these line settings since it does not vary; there is always only one start bit.

Data bit

The data bits represent the actual information that is being transmitted. In asynchronous communications it is normal to have either seven or eight data bits in each unit transmitted. The number of data bits used will normally be related to the parity setting which is explained below.

In terms of actual operation there is no difference between seven or eight data bits for the transmission of text files. In certain circumstances, however, a setting of eight data bits will be required for the transmission of non-text binary files (see page 92). Examples of binary files are: word processing files, spreadsheet data files and computer programs.

Stop bit

There is normally one stop bit used to mark the end of each unit. Old systems running at slow speeds may require two stop bits.

Parity bit

The concept of the parity bit is relatively complicated. Some microcomputers use a system called 'parity checking' in order to ensure that none of the bits in a byte become corrupted when it is moved around in the memory of the computer. The principle of parity checking is quite ingenious. The eight data bits stored by any one byte are, of course, composed entirely of 1s and 0s. The sum total of this collection of bits must, necessarily, either be odd or even. If any one bit is altered from a 1 to a 0 or from a 0 to a 1 then the sum of the group of bits will, as a consequence, change from odd to even or from even to odd.

A microcomputer that uses parity checking is fitted with some extra silicon chips which, in effect, add to each byte a ninth bit — the parity bit. A given microcomputer may be functioning using even or odd parity. Let us assume we are working with even parity. The computer will set the parity bit which accompanies each byte so that the sum total of all eight bits in the byte plus the parity bit is always even. If the total of the eight data bits is an odd number then the parity bit will be set to 1 so that the total of all the bits is an even number. If the total of the eight data bits is an even number then the parity bit will be set to 0 so that the total of all the bits remains an even number. Each time a byte is moved around inside the computer a quick check is carried out to make sure that the total of the parity bit plus the eight bits in the byte is still an even number. If any one of the bits has been corrupted then the total will be an odd number and the system will register a fault. Of course if two bits within the same byte are simultaneously corrupted then the parity check will not work — but this is unlikely. Nowadays, parity checking is used in some top-end microcomputers but most cheap PC-style computers do not use it.

The principle of parity checking can also be used in other situations. In certain circumstances it is possible to set up a computer and printer so that the printer carries out a parity check on each byte before it is printed. If a parity error is detected then a distinctive character such as a * is printed. In this case the parity check is used simply to warn that a problem has occurred.

Parity bit settings are still encountered in data communications — even when the transmission is between two computers that do not themselves use parity checking. It is nonetheless essential that both computers are set to the same parity, otherwise the transmission will be garbled.

If a parity bit is specified in data communications then one of the eight bits in a normal byte must be used as the parity bit. Only the seven remaining bits in the byte are available to carry data. The effect of this is that only 128 (ie 2^7) characters are available rather than the full 256 (ie 2^8) characters of the normal eight bit ASCII table. The first half of the ASCII table contains all the characters required for normal text transmission. Using only seven data bits, however, it will not be possible to transmit messages containing characters in the second half of the ASCII table, such as the Greek letters used in scientific equations. Parity checking on the transmission of a normal text message actually makes very little sense. A parity check can register that a fault has occurred but it cannot correct the fault. A user who is sending a text message will not need to be informed that a sentence like 'the cat sat on the !*"&' has been corrupted. That is obvious.

There may be situations in which a parity bit is useful. For the transmission of text messages, however, the use of a parity bit is largely a matter of convention. Most modern systems use a line setting of eight data bits and no parity bit, which allows, among other things, the use of the whole ASCII character table.

Possible parity bit settings for data communication include even, odd and none (ie no parity bit is used). There are a couple of other jargon terms which may be encountered in the context of the parity bit: 'mark' and 'space'. Mark is a jargon term referring to the state of a data communications line which is in use but idle at that particular moment. Mark is always represented by a binary 1. Space, on the other hand, is always represented by a binary 0. A line setting might, for example, require seven data bits and parity set to space. This would mean that the eighth bit (which would have been the parity bit) always has a value of 0.

Speed of transmission

Data can be transmitted at various speeds. The speed of computer data transmissions is measured in bits per second (bps). Another term — baud — is often taken to mean the same as bits per second. The two terms are commonly used as if they were completely interchangeable, which is not strictly correct. There are some complicated technical arguments involved. In summary, baud is a term used in telecommunications jargon and is associated with the capabilities of modems and phone lines. Bits per second is a computer term. This book will stick to bits per second unless it is legitimate to use the term baud. In real life people are not so pedantic!

The most common transmission speeds used by microcomputers for sending data over the telephone network are: 300 bits per second, 1200 bps and 2400 bps. Frequently used communications settings require ten bits to transmit one byte. This may be one start bit, eight data bits and one stop bit or alternatively one start bit, seven data bits, one parity bit and one stop bit. One byte is used to represent one character. The above transmission speeds will, therefore, commonly be equivalent to 30 characters per second, 120 characters per second and 240 characters per second, respectively. For many e-mail users the choice of transmission speed will depend in part on the speeds offered by their local packet switching network. This is the data network offered by many national telecommunications companies. There is more about this in Chapter 7.

Local software settings

There are other variables which are set at the same time as the line settings: handshaking, duplex, line feed, and the serial port which is being used. These local software settings do not affect the ability of the distant computer to re-assemble the stream of incoming bits into coherent data. They are settings that affect the operation of the local computer.

Handshaking or flow control

Handshaking refers to a facility that allows a computer to request a pause during transmission. Say, for example, that a microcomputer is downloading (capturing to disc) a particularly long message. The data will be transmitted at a certain speed by the central host computer. It could be that the microcomputer is unable to keep up with the speed of the incoming data. Initially this will not be a problem. The backlog of incoming data will be stored in the memory of the microcomputer until it can be processed. The temporary storage area is known as a 'buffer'. If, however, the buffer becomes full then the microcomputer will have to send a message to the host requesting a pause in transmission. When some of the backlog has been processed the microcomputer will send another message requesting the resumption of transmission. This process is known as handshaking.

Handshaking may be controlled through hardware or through software. Between a computer and a printer, for example, handshaking is often controlled through hardware. In this case, two wires in the printer cable are designated to carry messages stopping or resuming transmission. In the case of a microcomputer communicating with an e-mail host computer, however, handshaking is controlled through software. This means that certain codes are defined which, when received, will cause either computer to pause or re-start transmission. The special codes most commonly used in software handshaking are a pair called XON and XOFF. These are drawn from the 32 special 'control codes' which are defined in the ASCII standard. Communications software packages will normally offer a choice between handshaking (also known as 'flow control') 'enabled' or 'disabled'. The normal setting for e-mail users is XON/XOFF handshaking enabled.

The XOFF code can in fact often be generated direct from the keyboard of a PC computer by holding down the key marked 'control' (or 'Ctrl') and typing an 'S'. Similarly, holding down the control key and typing a 'Q' generates XON. It is, therefore, possible for computer users to carry on their own 'handshaking' with their computer. Say, for example, that an e-mail message cannot be read because it is scrolling up the screen too fast. Holding down the control key and typing an S will 'freeze' the screen. The e-mail host receives an XOFF and consequently pauses. Typing control and Q will re-start the transmission. This trick is not restricted to e-mail. It works in many types of software package.

Duplex or echo

Duplex and echo are two separate terms but their use is

80

interrelated. Communications software packages commonly refer to duplex although some may use the term echo. There are two possible settings: full duplex and half duplex. These correspond to distant echo and local echo.

Full duplex (distant echo) is the normal setting for a microcomputer that is communicating with an e-mail host computer. Full duplex refers to a communications link that can carry data simultaneously in both directions (just as a telephone can carry voices in two directions at the same time). E-mail users always use duplex lines. Distant echo is a facility that takes advantage of full duplex operation to 'echo' characters back from the central host computer. Suppose a user is on-line (connected) to the e-mail host computer. The screen might be prompting the user to enter some information, for example their mailbox name. The user duly types in this information. As each letter is pressed on the keyboard it appears on the screen. When the microcomputer is set to distant echo, the character corresponding to the key that has been pressed is sent via the modem to the central host computer. When the host computer receives the information it sends it back to the personal computer again and it is then displayed on the screen. The advantage of this system is that the e-mail user has a clearer idea of what the central host is receiving. It is possible, for example, to see the effects of corruption due to line noise since this will appear on the screen as garbage. The interference may have occurred on the way out to the host computer or on the way back from the host computer to the microcomputer. If it occurred on the way back then the host computer will, of course, have received the original message correctly. In this case, the echo is useful simply as a guide to the general state of the line.

A half duplex line, on the other hand, is a communications link that can carry data in two directions but only in one direction at a time. This kind of communication may be encountered in the world of large mainframe and mini computers. In the case of half duplex transmission the personal computer will be set to local echo. It is not practical for characters to be echoed back (since the line only operates in one direction at a time). Instead, characters typed in at the keyboard of the personal computer are simply displayed directly on screen without going via the central host computer.

If duplex or echo is set incorrectly then text will either appear double on the screen or it will not appear at all.

Line feed/carriage return

'Line feed' and 'carriage return' are two of the special control codes defined in the ASCII standard. They are used to control the display on a computer screen or the operation of a printer. The effect of line feed is to move the cursor or print head one line down. Carriage return, on the other hand, returns the cursor or print head to the beginning of a line. When a printer has printed one line of text the paper is fed one line and the print head is returned to the left hand margin. The two commands line feed and carriage return are both executed. The two codes are normally used together so that some printers, for example, will automatically insert a line feed whenever a carriage return is encountered.

The communications software package of an e-mail user may be set to insert either a line feed or a line feed and a carriage return at the end of each line of incoming text. This will affect the screen display and any subsequent printout. The correct setting for the microcomputer will depend on whether or not the host computer inserts a carriage return at the end of each line. The normal setting for an e-mail user is line feed only but if the host computer does not insert carriage returns then the microcomputer will have to add both a line feed and a carriage return.

If neither the host nor the personal computer is inserting a carriage return then the text received from the host will appear as a continuous string on one line without ever 'wrapping' on to the following lines. This is inconvenient since it will not be possible to read the message on the screen. If, however, the message is also being saved to disc then the process of downloading will not be affected. Indeed, in certain cases it can even be advantageous to capture a message to disc without added carriage returns. It may subsequently be easier to retrieve and re-format the text in a word processing package.

If, on the other hand, the host and the personal computer are both inserting carriage returns then an extra blank line will appear between each line of text. In this case it will be possible to read the message on the screen but difficult to reformat it in a word processing package.

Serial port

The personal computer may have more than one serial port (socket). If this is the case it will be necessary to ensure that the communications software is transmitting the data to the serial port to which the modem is attached.

In computer jargon two serial ports are referred to as COM1 and COM2 respectively. The communications software will offer some simple means of specifying which should be used. There is often no visible means of telling the two apart. Trial and error with the software settings is normally the quickest way of finding out which serial port the modem is attached to. The modem will not register any activity at all if the computer is sending data to the wrong serial port.

Examples of line settings

Poptel/GeoNet and GreenNet are the main progressive e-mail networks in Britain. GreenNet requires eight data bits, no parity bit and one stop bit. GeoNet can be accessed using the same line settings or using seven data bits, even parity and one stop bit. These are two of the most common settings. In both cases the software on the microcomputer should be set to distant echo and line feed only. The speed of transmission will depend on the modem of the user and the local packet switching network (see Chapter 7). Most packet switching networks allow access at 300 bits per second and 1200 bps. Some will also offer the 'split speed' setting, 1200/75 bps (see page 63). Advanced systems will also have an option for access at 2400 bps.

In addition, it is possible to call many of the e-mail systems direct, without using packet switching. This may be particularly useful for subscribers in developing countries that do not have packet switching. The normal options for direct dial access to an e-mail system are 300 bps, 1200 bps and 2400 bps.

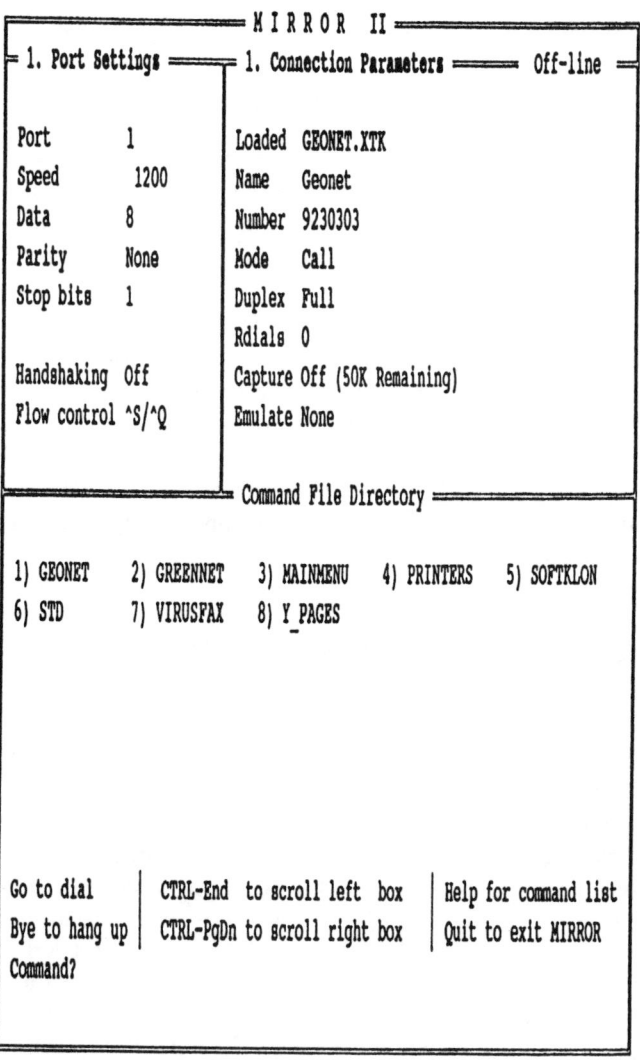

```
================ M I R R O R   II ================
= 1. Port Settings ====== 1. Connection Parameters ======= Off-line =


    Port       1          Loaded  GEONET.XTK
    Speed      1200        Name    Geonet
    Data       8           Number  9230303
    Parity     None        Mode    Call
    Stop bits  1           Duplex  Full
                           Rdials  0
    Handshaking  Off       Capture Off (50K Remaining)
    Flow control ^S/^Q     Emulate None

                      = Command File Directory =

    1) GEONET    2) GREENNET    3) MAINMENU    4) PRINTERS    5) SOFTKLON
    6) STD       7) VIRUSFAX    8) Y_PAGES






    Go to dial    | CTRL-End  to scroll left  box | Help for command list
    Bye to hang up | CTRL-PgDn to scroll right box | Quit to exit MIRROR
    Command?
```

Figure 6: *Main Mirror screen* This is the main screen from the Mirror II software package. The line settings or "port settings" are ready for a direct dial call to Poptel/GeoNet. The settings can be saved to disc and retrieved as required. They can be altered by entering simple commands at the 'Command' prompt. Pushing return will cause Mirror to begin dialling GeoNet.

```
              DIALING   DIRECTORY

            Name            Number      Baud P D S   E
    1- GeoNet (direct dial)      9230303    2400-N-8-1   N
    2- GeoNet (via PSS)      081-840-5500   1200-E-7-1   N
    3- GeoNet (via Dialplus)     490-2200   2400-E-7-1   N
    4- GreenNet (via Dialplus)   490-2200   2400-S-7-1   N
    5- Russell Press         012-345-6789   1200-N-8-1   N
    6- Virus Fax International 098-765-4321 2400-N-8-1   N
    7- Electronic Yellow Pages  01-222-3344 1200-N-8-1   N
    8- ......................   . ... ...-....  1200-N-8-1   N
    9- ......................   . ... ...-....  1200-N-8-1   N
   10- ......................   . ... ...-....  1200-N-8-1   N


   ==>      R Revise       M Manual Dialing    Entry to Dial
            P LD Codes     D Delete Entry      F Find
            PgUp/PgDn Page L Print Entries     ↑/↓ Scroll
            Home Top Page  End Bottom Page     ESC Exit


   Modem command: ATDP              LD Codes Active:


                        AUTO  DIALER
```

Figure 7: *Procomm dialling directory* A series of telephone numbers can be stored in the Procomm dialling directory together with their associated line settings. See page 86.

How to set up the modem and computer

The modem and the computer are usually set up using the communications software package. The settings are either selected through a menu system or by issuing some simple commands. It is possible to save the required settings to disc so that the microcomputer is automatically configured correctly each time the communications package is used. It is also possible to save different telephone numbers and their associated line settings in some form of 'dialling directory'. When a number is selected from the dialling directory, the microcomputer is automatically configured to the correct settings before the appropriate number is dialled (see Figure 7).

Sending and reading messages

6

This chapter begins by examining plain text transmissions — the most common form of traffic on an e-mail network. It then goes on to examine situations in which a plain text transmission is not appropriate. Such situations include the transmission of word processing files and the transmission of other kinds of binary data files. In these cases a file transfer protocol, such as X-modem or Kermit, must be used. After examining these protocols, the chapter ends by looking at error correction techniques, such as MNP and V42.

Plain text ASCII messages

The most common method of swapping messages on an e-mail system is through plain ASCII text messages. Plain ASCII text is, in effect, the lowest common denominator for microcomputers. Correspondents swapping plain text messages can be confident that there will not be any major problems of incompatibility. The sender does not have to worry which microcomputer or word processing package the recipient is using — they will be able to deal with ASCII.

The ASCII standard, it will be recalled, is like an 'alphabet' for microcomputers. Different characters are assigned to the different possible values of a byte. The ASCII code covers the letters of the alphabet, the numbers 0 to 9, punctuation marks and other special characters, such as '*'. In addition to these printable 'text' characters, the ASCII standard also defines 32 special 'control codes'. These are not like normal text characters. Instead, they are used to control the functioning of the computer or printer. Some of these control codes may be used in normal text files. The 'carriage return' and 'line feed' codes, for example, cause text to be displayed at the beginning of a new line on the screen or to be printed at the beginning of a new line by a printer. The carriage return code is generated by pressing the 'return' key on a normal computer keyboard. Other control codes, however, will be interpreted in different ways by different software packages. The effect of these codes will vary in different situations.

A plain ASCII text message is a message which consists entirely of normal text characters plus any standard control codes, such as the carriage return code. A binary file, on the other hand, contains data that is not intended to be read as ASCII text. Instead, it might contain non-ASCII, non-text, coded information intended for use directly by the computer or by a specific computer program. Examples of binary files are computer programs, software packages and spreadsheet data files. A spreadsheet is a software package that offers a method for storing and manipulating numeric or financial information.

Creating a plain ASCII text file

A user sending a short e-mail message of a few lines will simply log on (connect up) with the e-mail system and type in the text directly from the keyboard whilst on-line. For longer messages, however, the text should normally be prepared beforehand and saved to disc using a word processing package. This saves time and money. E-mail users normally swap plain text messages, so the prepared file will probably have to be a plain ASCII text file.

Files created by word processing packages — such as WordPerfect and Wordstar — are not plain ASCII text files. Besides the normal text information, such word processing files may also contain non-ASCII binary code and special control codes. These non-text codes are used to regulate features such as text-enhancement and page formatting. Bold and underlined text, indented text, page numbering, headers and footers are all examples of such enhancements. Different word processing packages deal with these additional features in different — and incompatible — ways. All word processing packages will, however, offer some simple method for creating and retrieving plain ASCII text files. The exact procedure will vary between packages. Individual users will have to determine how their particular word processing package handles ASCII files.

In this context, creating an ASCII text file means stripping from a word processing file all of the non-text binary code and special control characters so that only normal text characters remain.

ASCII text file transfer

As described above, e-mail users will normally key in their messages, and save them to disc as ASCII text files, before logging on (connecting up) to the e-mail system. When a connection has been established, the e-mail user will issue the appropriate commands to send a message to a given mailbox or boxes. The nature of these commands will depend on which e-mail system is being used. At an appropriate point, the text of the message will have to be entered. The user could simply begin typing text from the keyboard. Alternatively, he or she could command the communications software package to begin uploading (sending) a specified ASCII file direct from disc. The exact commands to upload a file will vary between different software packages. The text will be 'echoed' back to microcomputer as it is sent to the central host computer so the user will see the message scrolling up the screen. When the ASCII text-file transfer is complete the user may, if desired, type additional comments. The central host computer does not make any distinction between incoming ASCII text sent direct from a disc and incoming ASCII text entered at the keyboard. When all is ready the user must indicate to the host computer that input is complete. The central host computer should then confirm that the message has been successfully sent.

Binary file transfers

ASCII is invaluable as a common 'language' for microcomputers. There are, however, circumstances in which it is preferable to send non-text, non-ASCII files by e-mail.

It can, for example, be upsetting to see carefully formatted documents — with section headings, indented paragraphs and fancy font changes — turned into a sheet of plain ASCII text. Even underline and bold are stripped from ASCII files. The transmission of characters with accents may also cause some problems due to the existence of different national 'dialects' of ASCII. E-mail members who use the same word processing package may therefore be inclined to transfer the original word processing files direct rather than convert the message into ASCII at one end and then back out of ASCII again at the other. In this way all page formatting, print enhancements, non-English characters and so on can be preserved. It might, for example, be appropriate to arrange a direct transfer of word processing files between different branches of the same organisation, provided, of course, that they are all standardised on the same word processing package.

E-mail users may also sometimes wish to swap other kinds of non-text, binary files. Different branches of an organisation might, for example, all store financial information using the same spreadsheet package. With careful preparation it would be possible for all the branches to send their spreadsheets via e-mail to a central office where they could be consolidated into one set of overall figures.

Binary files — containing non-ASCII, non-text data — cannot be transmitted in the same way as normal ASCII files. This is because the receiving computer is set up to expect incoming text data. The transmission of data containing ASCII control codes could be misinterpreted by the receiving computer. To avoid these problems a file transfer protocol must be used, as described below.

File transfer protocols

The basic principle of all file transfer protocols is similar. The file to be sent is transmitted in small blocks. Before each block is sent, the communications software will perform a mathematical calculation. In the simplest form, this calculation involves adding together all the data bits in each block. The result of this addition is known as the 'checksum'. The block is then transmitted together with the checksum. The receiving computer will carry out the same mathematical calculation on the block. If the result does not tally with the checksum then corruption has occurred during transmission. In this case a message is returned to the sending computer requesting that the last block should be re-sent. Otherwise an acknowledgement of error-free reception is returned.

Two of the special ASCII control codes — ACK and NAK — are used for acknowledgement and 'negative acknowledgment'. Each block is transmitted in this way until the whole file has been received without corruption.

Most modern file transfer protocols use mathematical calculations that are more complex than simple addition. These reduce the risk of any corruption slipping through undetected. The principle of re-sending corrupted blocks remains the same.

File transfer protocols offer two distinct benefits. Firstly, a file will almost certainly be transmitted entirely error free, thanks to the re-sending of corrupted blocks. Secondly, a file transfer protocol enables the transmission of non-text, non-ASCII files. As mentioned above, the straight transmission of data containing non-text control codes is problematic since these control codes may be acted upon by the receiving computer, instead of simply being treated as incoming data. When a file is transferred using a file transfer protocol, however, the stream of data is broken into blocks of pre-determined size. In this case, the receiving computer is not expecting a steady stream of text data but rather a stream of regular sized blocks of data. The receiving computer will not 'look' inside the blocks of data. It does not matter if the incoming blocks of data contain control codes as the receiving computer will not act on them, but will simply reconstruct the original file from the separate blocks.

In order for an e-mail member to use a file transfer protocol the communications software in use on the microcomputer must offer a technique that is also offered by the e-mail system. By far the most popular file transfer protocols in the field of e-mail are a pair called X-modem and Kermit.

X-modem

X-modem is an old file transfer protocol that uses the checksum addition technique outlined above. There is a improved version of X-modem, which uses a more advanced mathematical technique called Cyclic Redundancy Check or CRC.

X-modem requires line settings of eight data bits, no parity and one stop bit. Standard X-modem transmits blocks of 128 bytes at a time. Using standard X-modem it is possible to transfer only one file per command. In other words, reading six e-mail messages would require six separate X-modem commands. It is not possible to transmit a group of files in a single operation.

There are a number of variations on the original X-modem file transfer protocol. Modem-7, for example, can work with a line setting of seven data bits while Y-modem can work with larger block sizes thereby increasing the effective transmission speed. There is also a variant of Y-modem which allows groups of files to be transmitted with a single command. The average e-mail user will not, however, generally be concerned with the pros and cons of these different variants. The one important question will be: which file transfer protocols does the e-mail system offer? Frequently, this will simply be standard X-modem.

Kermit

Kermit is the name of a communications software package and also of a file transfer protocol. It is available cheaply, or free, through public sources. The package is very useful. It offers normal communications software facilities and also includes the Kermit file transfer protocol. Other communications packages, for example Procomm, also offer the Kermit file transfer protocol as an option.

Together with X-modem, Kermit is the file transfer protocol most commonly offered by e-mail systems. One advantage of Kermit is that it allows the transmission of binary (non-text) files on seven-bit systems. In other words, Kermit can work with a line setting of either seven or eight data bits whereas standard X-modem can only operate with a setting of eight data bits. There are certain situations in which it may be necessary to operate with a line setting of seven data bits. In these cases an e-mail subscriber wishing to send or receive non-text, binary files will have to use Kermit.

Using file transfer protocols

Popular communications software packages, such as Procomm and Mirror, offer a wide range of file transfer protocols including X-modem, Y-modem and Kermit. APC e-mail systems, such as PeaceNet and GreenNet, support both X-modem and Kermit while the GeoNet e-mail system supports X-modem and Y-modem (see page 37 for details of the different e-mail systems).

SENDING AND READING MESSAGES

The method for sending a file using X-modem or Kermit will normally be quite similar to the standard procedure for sending a text message. It is, however, only possible to transmit complete files using these protocols (hence the name 'file transfer protocols').

Taking the GeoNet e-mail network as an example, a user who is sending a non-text file will call up the system in the normal way. Next they issue a simple command to the GeoNet host computer indicating that they wish to send a message using the X-modem file transfer protocol. After specifying the recipient, they are given the chance to enter a text message. This may be used to explain to the recipient that there follows a binary file (such as a computer program or a spreadsheet). When the text message is complete the central host computer prompts the user to begin the X-modem transfer. The actual transfer is started by the user instructing the communications software on the personal computer to begin uploading (sending) a specified file using X-modem. X-modem reception begins automatically when the e-mail host computer registers that X-modem has been started on the microcomputer. The message will not appear on the screen (it may not be a text message anyway). The communications software will, however, indicate that transmission is in progress. This is often done by providing a running commentary on the percentage of the file that has been successfully transmitted. The GeoNet host computer will receive the file using X-modem. When transmission is complete the user may proceed as usual.

The GeoNet central host computer monitors the file during X-modem transmission. If the message consists entirely of normal text characters then it is simply deposited in the mailbox of the recipient in the normal way. The recipient will be unaware of the fact that the message was transmitted to the host using X-modem. The sender, however, can be happy in the certainty that it was transmitted without corruption. If, on the other hand, the file is a binary file — containing non-text, ASCII control codes — the GeoNet host will register this fact. It will place the transmission in the mailbox of the recipient with a note indicating that it is a binary file (ie a non-text file) which must be downloaded (captured to disc) using a file transfer protocol.

To download a binary file the recipient issues the 'read' command in the normal way. Any initial text message entered by the sender will appear on the screen. Next the e-mail host computer will prompt the user to begin the file transfer. At this point, the user must instruct the communications software on the personal computer to download (capture) a file using X-modem. The central host computer will again automatically begin sending the X-modem file when it registers that X-modem has been started on the microcomputer.

It is important to note the sequence when reading a file using X-modem. First the e-mail host computer is instructed to send a file using X-modem, then the communications software package on the microcomputer is instructed to receive a file using X-modem. Not vice versa.

The recipient will not see the file on the screen while it is being sent. When complete, the recipient terminates the X-modem download and proceeds as normal.

Line noise

As mentioned above, file transfer protocols can be used to ensure error free transmission. This is useful in situations where corruption due to line noise is a persistent problem. A little line noise while sending or reading ordinary, short ASCII text messages will not normally be disastrous. The text will be slightly corrupted but it should still be possible to understand the message, filling in a few missing letters or words if necessary. It is simple enough to download (read) a short message again, if it is really unintelligible. For longer messages, however, line noise may be a source of great frustration. There is nothing more annoying than to reach page 12 of a 14-page transmission only to see a vital paragraph transformed into a string of garbage by crackling on the line. The whole message will have to be re-read wasting time and money.

Corruption due to line noise can also occasionally have the effect of terminating the process of capturing to disc. It may appear that text is being downloaded (captured to disc) quite normally. Subsequent inspection, however, will reveal that the last part of the message is missing from the capture file.

Line noise may prove no more than an occasional irritation with short messages but with longer files it can be a real problem and source of frustration. One answer may be to encourage your partners to split their transmissions into several shorter messages. This makes it easier to re-read messages affected by line noise. Alternatively, longer documents can be sent or read using a file transfer protocol — even if they are plain text files. Using a file transfer protocol will help to ensure that messages are sent or read error-free. A third possibility is to use an error-correcting modem which eliminates line noise altogether.

Error correction techniques

Kermit and X-modem are file transfer protocols which provide error correction. They are not true error correction techniques. Error correction is more comprehensive than a file transfer protocol, offering protection for the entire duration of a session on-line with the central host computer, not just during the actual transmission of a file. Error correction techniques do, nonetheless, operate on the same principle as file transfer protocols. A transmission is divided into blocks and a check is applied to each block before it is transmitted. A similar check is applied by the receiver and corrupted blocks are re-sent until they are received error free.

File transfer protocols like Kermit and X-modem are software-based. This means that the user must have a software package that offers these particular protocols. Error correction techniques, on the other hand, can be hardware-based, whereby the necessary software and memory are actually built in to the modem. An error-correcting modem will be more expensive than an equivalent modem without error correction. Alternatively, some error correction techniques can also be implemented through software, which means that a software package regulates the error correction. In order to use a given error correction technique, an e-mail user must buy a modem or a software package which offers that technique and — just as importantly — the distant system must use exactly the same error correction technique. In the case of e-mail users, the 'distant system' may refer either to the exchange of a packet switching system (see Chapter 7) or to a modem attached to the e-mail host computer, depending on which method of access is being used.

The use of error correction may seem like a lot of trouble and expense for little benefit. The secret behind the importance of error correction lies in the fact that these techniques allow faster transmission speeds. Transmission without error correction at speeds greater than 1200 bits per second may be problematic on noisy public telephone lines, since line noise becomes progressively more disruptive at higher transmission speeds. Even simple error correction makes transmission at 2400 bits per second feasible (provided, of course, that the modem can operate at this speed). For users struggling with noisy phone lines at 1200 bps, on-line time (and on-line charges) can be halved by using a 2400 bps error-correcting modem.

It is common for error correction techniques to be combined with data compression techniques. These are complicated, mathematically-based systems for reducing the actual number of bits used to transmit a given quantity of data. For example, the most commonly used characters (a,e,i etc) can be represented by shorter bit patterns (ie fewer than seven bits) while the less frequently used ones (x,q,z etc) are represented by longer sequences. Another data compression technique involves the elimination of repetitive character strings. Instead, for example, of sending a string of 58 spaces, a much shorter code, indicating 58 x (space), may be transmitted. At this level, the good old picture of start bits, data bits, stop bits and the ASCII standard no longer applies during the actual data transmission.

Data compression increases the effective rate of transmission since fewer bits are needed to transmit a given quantity of data. It may have a dramatic impact on the transmission of text files but will be less effective in the transmission of other types of binary file.

MNP

One of the most commonly used error correction techniques is MNP, which stands for Microcom Networking Protocol. Microcom is the modem manufacturer that developed and owns

96

the MNP error correction technique. MNP is used by other modem manufacturers under licence. There are nine levels of MNP starting with level 1 as the most simple. Levels 1 to 5 might be relevant to the needs of small organisations. Modems offering MNP levels 6 to 9 are too expensive and sophisticated to be of interest to normal e-mail users.

Level 1 relates to half-duplex operation which is not relevant to e-mail. Level 2 covers full duplex, asynchronous data transmission which is the norm for e-mail users (covered in Chapter 5). The error correction technique employed in level 2 is similar to a normal file transfer protocol. A 2400 bits per second modem using MNP level 2 will only transfer data at around 2000 bps, a reduction in performance which is due to the extra bits that must be transmitted for error checking. MNP level 3 relates to synchronous transmission and is not, therefore, relevant to e-mail.

Level 4 has techniques to regulate the size of the packets of data transmitted, and to reduce the number of bits used to control the actual transmission. On a good line larger packets of data are used, thereby increasing the effective rate of data transmission. On a poorer line the size of the packets is reduced, making it quicker to re-send corrupted packets. These techniques increase the effective rate of data transmission by reducing the amount of time wasted both in sending the bits that control the data transmission and the bits that are used to check for errors. The maximum notional throughput for a 2400 bits per second modem is 240 characters (ie bytes) per second. This is assuming that ten bits are needed to transmit each byte (one start bit, eight data bits and one stop bit). Using MNP level 4, however, the actual data throughput may be increased to around 290 characters per second on a good line.

MNP level 5 adds data compression techniques. The effect of these techniques will vary depending on the type of file being sent. Transmission at level 5 may double the data throughput rate for an ordinary text file. It will also greatly increase the speed of transmission for a word processing file. It will, however, have little effect on the transmission of binary files such as spreadsheet data files or computer programs.

Modems offering MNP will always work together, but only at the highest level offered by the less sophisticated of the pair. An

MNP modem will, of course, work with a normal modem — but without offering any error correction. MNP is normally built in to the modem, but there is a growing tendency for software packages to offer MNP error correction. With this kind of software package it is possible to use an ordinary modem and still benefit from MNP error correction. An example of such a software package is Mirror III (not Mirror II), which provides MNP to class 5.

CCITT V42

CCITT is a highly influential body, connected with the United Nations, which defines international standards in the field of telecommunications. V42 is a standard — ratified in 1989 — that relates to error correction for modems. Sections of the CCITT wanted to base the error correction standard for modems on a technique derived from something called LAP (Link Access Protocol). LAP is used to provide error correction in packet switching networks (see Chapter 7). The LAP error correction for modems uses a completely different technique from that used in MNP. However, the large community of existing MNP users could not be ignored when formulating the new standard for error correction in modems. The result was a classic committee compromise whereby the main V42 error correction specification uses a derivative of Link Access Protocol called LAPM (LAP for modems), while an appendix to the main text supports MNP. In order for a modem to be fully compliant with the V42 standard it must support LAPM as well as MNP to level 4. The area of MNP is, however, 'frozen'. All future developments of the V42 standard will be based on LAPM. CCITT has recently also produced a recommendation, known as V42 bis, relating to data compression for modems. V42 bis is not compatible with the data compression techniques defined in MNP level 5.

The CCITT has no 'enforcement' role. It simply recommends standards. Market forces decide whether a particular standard is adopted or forgotten. At present, V42 modems are a good deal more expensive than modems offering MNP up to level 5.

The telephone network 7

Packet switching: introduction

Many e-mail users connect up with their e-mail host computer via a packet switching system rather than by dialling direct to the central computer. Packet switching is a system for cheap and efficient data transmission. Public packet switching systems may be offered by national telecommunications bodies or large private companies, and will often work out cheaper for users who cannot contact the e-mail system with a local telephone call. Those users who are geographically remote from the central host computer may be able to connect up with the national packet switching system through a local call. They can then send data to the e-mail host computer via the packet switching system. The user will be charged a certain amount for the use of packet switching but the combined cost of the local telephone call to gain access to the packet switching system and the packet switching charges will normally be less than the cost of a direct middle or long-distance telephone call.

Public packet switching systems are sometimes referred to as Public Data Networks. All developed countries have at least one public packet switching system. Packet switching is now available in an ever increasing number of developing countries. All of the various national packet switching systems are linked in an international packet switching system, that is the backbone of international e-mail. An e-mail member will, via the international packet switching system, be able to connect up with a host computer in a different country at a cost which is less than the price of an equivalent international voice telephone call.

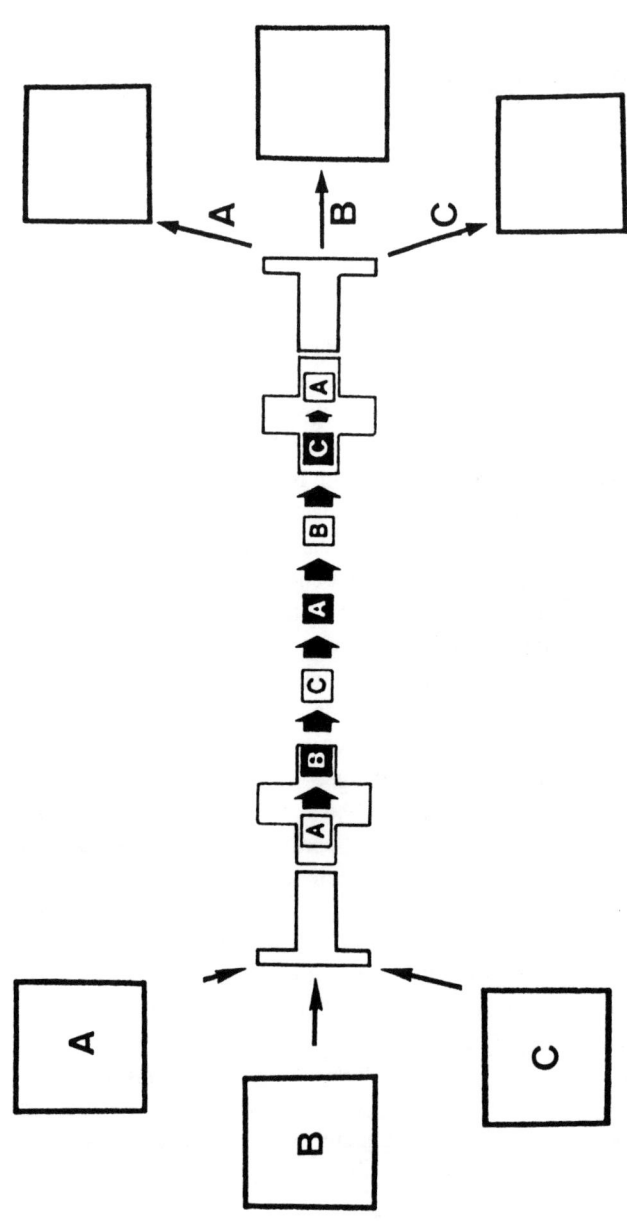

Figure 8: *Packets of data sharing a line* Packet switching is economical because data from many users can share the same line.

Packet switching: how it works

The term 'packet switching network' refers to a group of communications terminals linked as a matrix and capable of exchanging data according to certain standard rules. The network, or matrix of packet switching terminals, may either be public or private. A public packet switching network is a national system run by a state-owned or large private telecommunications company. In this case the 'communications terminals' are Packet Switching Exchanges, like telephone exchanges, situated in different towns and joined together by special high-speed, high-capacity communications links. A private packet switching network, on the other hand, can link computers in the different offices of a large corporation using private, leased communications lines.

The standard that defines the rules governing data exchange on a packet network is called X25, so packet switching networks may also be referred to as X25 networks. The X25 standard was developed in the early 1980s by CCITT, a highly influential organisation linked to the United Nations, which develops international standards for telecommunications. Nobody is 'forced' to use the X25 standard. In many circumstances, however, it is beneficial for all concerned to use a standard that has been adopted worldwide.

Data being transmitted across the network is first broken down into discrete packets by the packet switching terminal sending the data. Each packet might contain 128 bytes of data — that is to say, 128 characters. The packet switching terminal which is receiving the transmission will reconstruct the incoming packets into a coherent stream of data. Checks are carried out by the packet switching terminals that are sending and receiving the data to make sure that none of the packets are corrupted during transmission. A corrupted packet is re-sent until it is received error free. Messages confirming receipt of each packet or requesting re-transmission are swapped between the different packet switching terminals on the packet switching network. The X25 standard specifies the precise details governing the transfer of the packets.

PART TWO: TECHNICAL

In order to transfer data over a packet switching network, a computer must be able to construct and re-assemble packets of data in accordance with the rules laid down by the X25 standard. A computer able to do this is known as a 'packet terminal'. A normal microcomputer used for e-mail does not have these capabilities. A microcomputer, it will be recalled, transmits data asynchronously, and cannot act as 'packet terminal' without modification. For a simple micro to send data across a packet network, the asynchronous data must first be converted into X25 packets.

On public networks, entrance points into the packet switching network are provided by Packet Switching Exchanges (PSEs) situated in most major cities. These have various telephone numbers that can be dialled by a normal microcomputer using a modem. At the PSE there is a device called a Packet Assembler Disassembler (PAD). The PAD converts the asynchronous data coming from the microcomputer into packets for transmission on the packet switching network, and vice versa. The central host computer of an e-mail system will have its own PAD that connects it directly to the packet switching network. The PAD will be able to deal with several incoming calls simultaneously.

The reason for the development of packet switching is simple: it makes more efficient use of the communications network. An ordinary voice telephone call will include many pauses and periods of silence. The people involved are using one whole line even when nothing is being said. On a packet switching system, by contrast, the discrete packets of data from one user are 'woven in' with packets of data from many other sources. Several users share the same line thereby enabling modern high-capacity links to be used very efficiently. The analogy of logs being floated down a river illustrates the idea of packets sharing a line. This is one reason why data transmission via packet switching is cheaper than voice transmission over a telephone line.

Additionally, packet switching allows the system managers some control over the route that messages take over a network. If one particular exchange is faulty or overloaded, then it will be possible to re-direct traffic. Economical usage of the system can thus be maximised.

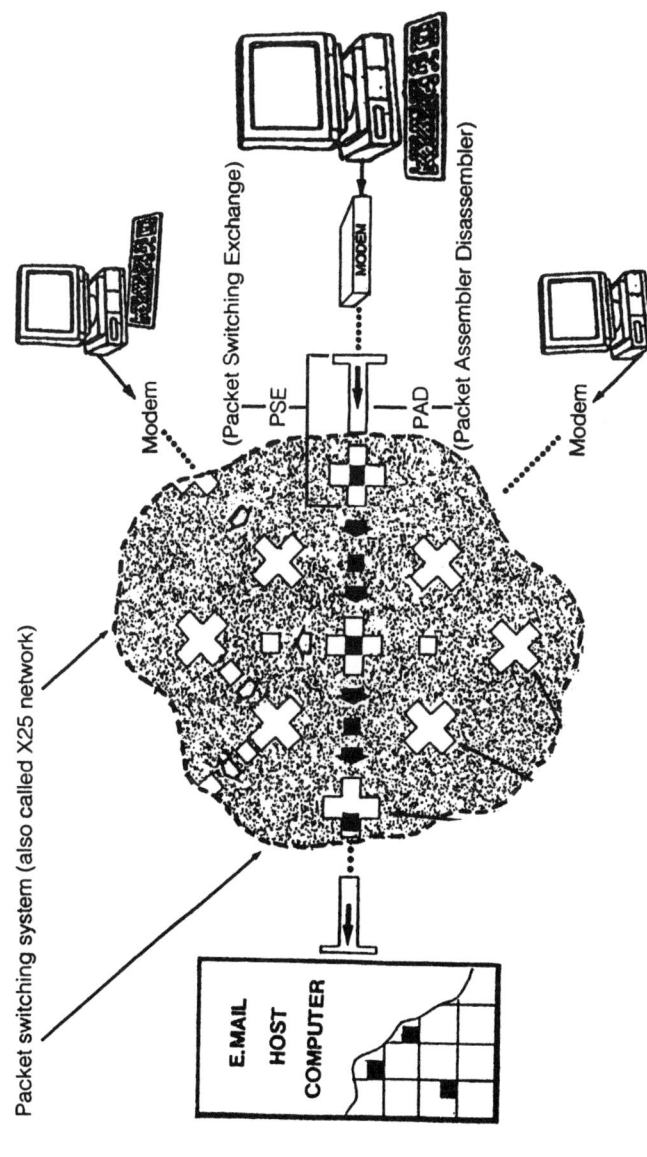

Figure 9: *Packet switching network*

PART TWO: TECHNICAL

Packet switching: a user's perspective

From the perspective of an e-mail user, packet switching initially involves a certain amount of bureaucracy and research. This includes joining the system, understanding the charging system, getting an NUI, establishing which PSE to use and finding the NUA of the e-mail host. All of these steps are explained below. Once these hurdles have been overcome and the system is running smoothly, there should not be any further need to worry about packet switching — except for the quarterly bills! Nonetheless, the time involved in joining a packet switching network should not be underestimated, particularly where a lot of bureaucracy is involved.

In some developing countries NGOs will be more advanced in the use of e-mail and packet switching than the commercial sector. Workers from the non-commercial sector may find that it is they, together with the local telecommunications company, who are the pioneers in exploring the possibilities of international communications. This can be exciting. It can also be slow.

Joining the packet switching network
In order to use packet switching a microcomputer user must be a member of the local packet switching network. This will involve signing some sort of contract with the telecommunications company. Joining the packet switching system is quite separate from joining the e-mail network (but see below for an exception).

The telecommunications company will provide potential users with a scale of charges. Typically, call charges will be based both on the connect time and on the actual amount of data transmitted (but not on the distance over which the data is transmitted). The exact balance between connect charges and volume charges will vary between systems. On top of these charges there may also be a one-off joining fee and possibly a refundable deposit. Calls that are routed from one packet switching network to another using the international packet switching system are charged separately.

When the formalities of joining the packet switching network have been completed the new user will be presented with a

Network User Identity (NUI) and a list of telephone numbers for local Packet Switching Exchanges (PSEs).

Network User Identity (NUI)

The NUI normally combines a membership number and a password. A microcomputer user has to give his or her NUI each time the packet switching network is accessed. This stops unauthorised users from gaining access to the system. The NUI also enables the packet switching company to monitor usage and charge subscribers for costs incurred.

Some e-mail systems offer a 'reverse charge' NUI facility. New members of the e-mail system are given an NUI that actually belongs to the e-mail system. The packet switching company bills the e-mail system directly for the costs incurred through use of the NUI. The e-mail operator then adds an appropriate proportional charge to other system charges for each user. This total bill is sent to individual users. There is nothing to stop a member of an e-mail system from using their own individual NUI but the reverse charge NUI is attractive because users do not have to register with the packet switching system in order to use e-mail. In addition, they only receive one e-mail bill rather than two. The reverse charge NUI is, however, not available on all packet switching systems.

Packet Switching Exchanges (PSEs)

A subscriber to a packet switching system will require a list of local PSEs. These are the point of entry into the packet switching network for normal microcomputer users. The PSE contains a device known as a PAD (Packet Assembler Disassembler), which converts asynchronous microcomputer data into packets that are transmitted across the packet switching system. A PSE will provide different telephone numbers for access to packet switching at different transmission speeds. Most packet switching systems allow access at 300 and 1200 bits per second. Some provide a split speed option, 1200/75 bps (see page 63). Advanced systems will also offer access at 2400 bps.

For packet switching to be economical the PSE used by an e-mail subscriber must be local. For example, an e-mail user in Glasgow connecting up with a host computer in London will not place an inter-city call, but will instead dial the PSE in Glasgow. The user therefore only needs to make a local call in order to enter the packet switching network. The total cost of the call for the e-mail user in Glasgow will be the price of a local call plus the additional charges of the packet switching system. This will be less than the cost of an inter-city call.

The 'local' PSE of an e-mail user is not, however, always in the same city or even the same country. A member of an e-mail network in a developing country that does not have packet switching may be able to join the packet switching system of a neighbouring country. The total cost of a call to, for example, a host computer in London will consist of the cost of an international telephone connection to the neighbouring country and a charge for using the international packet switching system to send the data through to Britain. This will not be cheap, but it may still cost less than dialling London direct.

Network User Address (NUA)

The last step for a prospective user of packet switching is to find out the Network User Address (NUA) of the e-mail host computer. This information will be available from the people who run the e-mail system. The NUA is the address of a communications terminal on a packet switching network, like a telephone number. CCITT — the body responsible for the X25 standard governing packet switching — has also produced guidelines specifying a standard format for NUAs.

A normal national NUA is a nine-figure number. This may be preceded by a four-figure Data Network Identification Code (DNIC). The DNIC is like an international telephone code. It specifies the particular national system on which an NUA is situated. The last figure of the DNIC and the first figure of an NUA are one and the same. The total length of the DNIC plus NUA is therefore normally twelve digits. If required, an extra one or two digits can be added to the NUA. These are used to specify different 'devices' at a certain address. An e-mail system, for example, might have more than one computer available at a given NUA. The optional extra figures will specify to which particular machine a packet should be passed. For this reason, the actual length of an NUA may be between nine and eleven digits. Different national packet switching systems may also require that the actual NUA has an additional prefix of some kind. On PSS, the British packet switching system, national calls are prefixed 'A' while international calls are prefixed 'A9'. As an example let us take the NUA of the London-based GeoNet host computer on PSS, which is: A2123002920. The 'A' is a requirement of the British packet switching system rather than a part of the NUA. The final 0 in this NUA is an optional extra digit. The DNIC (Data Network Identity Code) of PSS is 2342. The last 2 of this number is the same as the first 2 of the NUA. The full address of the London-based GeoNet host on a foreign network is therefore 2342123002920, plus any prefix that the local packet switching system might require.

Using packet switching

The detail of connecting up to a packet switching network will vary between different systems. There are certain basic steps that are always necessary, but the order and the exact details of the commands will vary. The basic elements may also be prefixed or suffixed by other characters or digits specific to different systems.

The e-mail user must first connect up with the local PSE (Packet Switching Exchange). There are often different numbers for different modem speeds. On more advanced systems there may be one number for all speeds. When a connection has been established the user gets a chance to 'configure' the PAD (Packet Assembler Disassembler). This means that the user can set a number of variables in the operation of the PAD that is attached to the PSE. This may be important since the packet switching system is not only used by microcomputers but also by other types of computer terminal. Configuring the PAD ensures that it is working in the most efficient way for a given task, in this case e-mail.

Some systems store a number of 'profiles' that hold all the appropriate settings for common types of computer terminal.

107

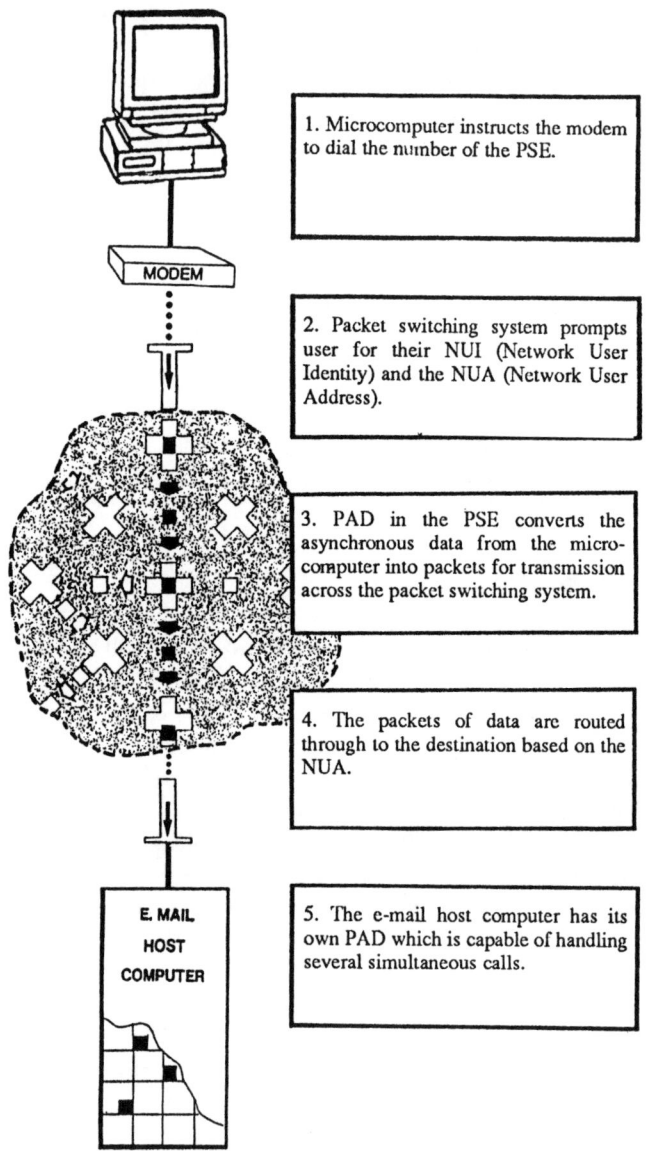

1. Microcomputer instructs the modem to dial the number of the PSE.

2. Packet switching system prompts user for their NUI (Network User Identity) and the NUA (Network User Address).

3. PAD in the PSE converts the asynchronous data from the microcomputer into packets for transmission across the packet switching system.

4. The packets of data are routed through to the destination based on the NUA.

5. The e-mail host computer has its own PAD which is capable of handling several simultaneous calls.

Figure 10: *The steps involved in establishing a call using packet switching*

On such systems the user can enter a simple code corresponding to their terminal type. The normal code for a microcomputer on the British packet switching system is: <RETURN> <RETURN>D1<RETURN>. On most systems the user will at this point see a reply from the packet switching system identifying the exchange being used. Next the user must give their NUI (Network User Identity), which will be about six characters long, followed, on some systems, by an additional password. Commonly the NUI or password do not appear on the screen as they are typed. This is to stop other people reading them. Assuming that the NUI and password are correct, the user must next give the NUA (Network User Address) of the host computer. The NUA will often be prefixed or suffixed by different codes for national or international calls. These codes vary from system to system. On some systems the whole string of NUI, password and NUA are entered as one line with a hyphen separating the NUA from the other elements. The packet switching system will confirm when a call has been established between the microcomputer and the e-mail host computer by repeating the NUA followed by '+COM'. After this, all communication will be directly with the e-mail host computer.

As the reader will now appreciate, packet switching is notorious for being difficult to use. Many packet switching systems are rectifying this situation by introducing more 'user friendly' menus and screens. In Britain, for example, the existing PSS service is being replaced by a new service called 'Dialplus'. A user need only dial in to the PSE (Packet Switching Exchange) and then type in a pre-arranged code, such as 'GREENNET', in order to be connected straight through to the required destination. The Dialplus service is faster than the older system, offering access up to 2400 bits per second. It also offers MNP error correction facilities for microcomputer users dialling in to the PSE.

Finally, it is worth repeating that, under normal circumstances, the operation of a packet switching system should be completely 'transparent' to an e-mail user. In other words, once a user has completed the necessary log in procedure the call should go straight through to the destination without any further bother. The user should not notice anything of the technicalities involved either on national or international calls.

Direct dial access to e-mail

The alternative to packet switching, when connecting up with an e-mail host, is to use direct dial access into the computer. Direct dial access is sometimes called 'dial up' access. The user does not bother with packet switching at all — but simply calls the host computer direct. Traditionally, the larger e-mail systems have been distinguished from smaller bulletin boards precisely because they offer access via the packet switching system. The larger e-mail systems have a PAD (Packet Assembler Disassembler) attached to the host computer, whereas smaller bulletin boards have an ordinary modem and can therefore only offer direct dial access.

Packet switching used to be preferable because it was cheaper — particularly for calls from overseas. By offering access via packet switching e-mail systems could hope to build up an international membership. The latest technological developments, however, have made this picture less clear-cut. The spread of error correction and data compression techniques (see page 95) has facilitated error-free, direct dial calls at greatly increased speeds. As an example, the Poptel/GeoNet host computer, which specialises in providing services to non-commercial users, has recently begun to offer direct dial access at 2400 bits per second with MNP error correction to level 5. MNP level 5, it will be recalled, is the level that offers data compression. A caller will, in theory at least, be able to achieve an effective data transfer rate approaching 480 characters per second after the data have been compressed, but in order to achieve this speed the e-mail user must have a 2400 bits per second modem offering MNP to class 5. In addition, the quality of the phone line must be reasonable if a high rate of data transfer is to be achieved.

The maximum access speed on some packet switching systems remains 1200 bits per second. Many systems are working on introducing 2400 bps access, but in some cases the development is slow. A user with a 2400 bps error correcting modem situated geographically close to the e-mail host may find it cheaper to use direct dial access rather than packet switching. The precise cost, however, will vary from case to case depending on usage and

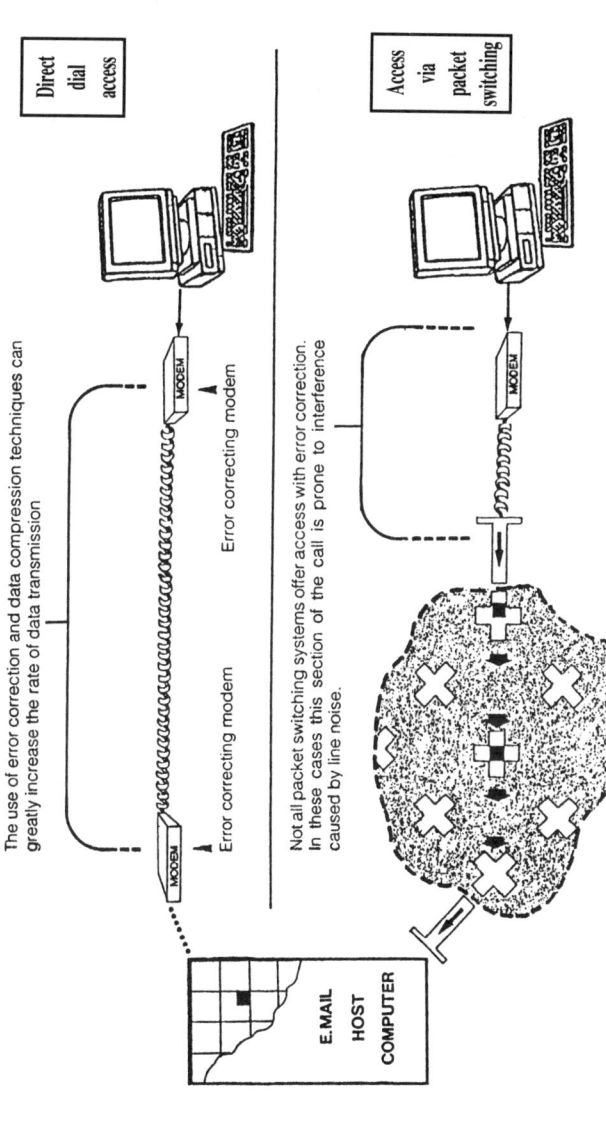

The use of error correction and data compression techniques can greatly increase the rate of data transmission

Error correcting modem

Error correcting modem

Error correcting modem

Not all packet switching systems offer access with error correction. In these cases this section of the call is prone to interference caused by line noise.

Direct dial access

Access via packet switching

MODEM

MODEM

MODEM

E.MAIL HOST COMPUTER

Figure 11: *Access to e-mail via direct dial and packet switching*

location. Direct dial access is also frequently used by subscribers in developing countries that do not have packet switching.

It is difficult to predict how the debate between direct dial and packet switching access will develop. On past form, the use of error correction and data compression in direct dial may spread and improve faster than the corresponding development of packet switching systems.

```
ATDP8405500
Connect

LO3\A006-1560040115
<Return><Return><Return>D1<Return>

NUI?
ngeonetxxxxxx

ADD?
a2123002920

2342123002920+COM

/// GeoNet "Value Added" Services - GEO2 ///

Name? ciir
Password? xxxxxxxx

Good afternoon, Welcome to Poptel!

Last call on: 09-07-90, 14:11:52
Monday, July 9, 1990, 15:00:48  (Port 2)

Please check the following bulletin-boards:

INDEX          (09-07-90)    ELISE-GB        (09-07-90)
NICARAGUA      (09-07-90)    FONDAD-BULLETIN (09-07-90)
PHILIPPINES    (09-07-90)


No. ST Date  Time  From/To     Lines  Subject

 5 RU 08-07 23:51 CIIR-HON       30  FOR GRAHAM FROM JOSINE
 8 RU 08-07 23:53 CIIR-HON       15  TO FINANCE FROM JOSINE
13 RU 09-07 13:27 CIIR-DR        27  *** BIN: GENDER & DEV
58 RU 09-07 14:08 ANTENNA-NL     48  E-MAIL BOOK
59 RU 09-07 14:37 ACCESS         27  COMMS SEMINAR

Command:
```

Figure 12: *Example of log in to GeoNet* (using old-style British Telecom Packet SwitchStream). The following information is supplied at various prompts: Network User Identity ('NGEONETXXXXX' for PSS), Network User Address of GeoNet ('A2123002920' for PSS), mailbox name ('CIIR' for GeoNet) and password ('XXXXXX' for GeoNet). For security reasons the last part of the NUI and the password do not appear on the screen. The bottom of the screen shows a list of unread messages waiting in the mailbox.

```
ATDP4902200
CONNECT

PSS Dialplus                    09-Jul-1990
          British Telecom
-------------------------------------------

              Welcome to

          P S S  D I A L P L U S

          Datacommunications made easy
          Reliable, cost-effective and error-free

-------------------------------------------
(C) British Telecommunications plc 1989


If problems occur, please telephone
0800 181555, quoting the following:
Clerkenwell 2      m01      MCPD2181

To access Dialplus, type your password
and press RETURN: xxxxxxxx
Calling    GREENNET
Connected to GREENNET

login: (? for help): CIIRLON
Password: (? for help): xxxxxxx
Terminal = capture (hit <RETURN> or enter terminal type):

    Welcome to GreenNet. For help, type "?"

You have new conf entries in nicanews gn.conferences help

You have new mail

GreenNet commands:(c)onf (h)elp (m)ail (s)etup (u)sers bye
?
```

Figure 13: *Example of log in to GreenNet* (using new-style
British Telecom Dialplus facilities). The first menu is the main
Dialplus screen. Typing GREENNET at the prompt takes the user
straight through to the GreenNet log in of mailbox name and
password. The bottom part of the screen lists the main GreenNet
commands. Each option leads to further sub-menus. The
arrangement of menus is similar on all APC e-mail systems.

The future

At the time of writing, the number of organisations and individuals using e-mail in the non-commercial sector is showing phenomenal growth. The field is vibrant with new projects and proposals. What will the future hold?

To begin with, there will be a growth in the use of on-line database services by non-commercial users. The initial step in this process is the introduction of an on-line database on the GeoNet and GreenNet e-mail systems using the Nigel software that is being developed by Antenna. The same facilities may be added to other e-mail hosts such as Alternex and the Web. Nigel software will also be available for small regional e-mail systems such as Worknet. In addition, Satis, the network of organisations working for sustainable development, is currently modifying the Nigel software for inclusion in the overall Satis Information System under the name of SatisFile.

Nigel software is not strictly speaking a database package but rather a 'software platform'. It is capable of directly importing and fully indexing data from a wide range of common database and word processing packages such as dBase and WordPerfect. It is, therefore, quite feasible to encourage the use of Nigel software within individual NGOs, since this does not require them to change the software they are using or to store the data in a standard form. Individual NGOs might have two specific uses for Nigel software. Firstly, it allows them to download files or records from other on-line services and then search them as an in-house database. Secondly, large NGOs that have their own databases could use Nigel to make these available to outside callers via a direct dial phone line.

The importance of on-line database services for NGOs has been emphasised throughout this book. The future will see the emergence of a broad range of NGO on-line services ranging from international and regional e-mail systems to individual NGO databases.

A second clear trend will be the continued development and expansion of NGO networks, with e-mail as one important tool in this process. The large Interdoc Conference 'Information Exchange for Social Change' held in the Netherlands in May 1990 has already given a boost to this on-going trend, bringing together organisations, networks and e-mail systems from around the world. It provided the opportunity for the development of the ideas, projects and personal contacts upon which the growth of networks depends.

Beyond these themes of databasing and networking, there are likely to be two other main trends: a continued expansion of services both in terms of size and quality, and a continued integration of different types of services.

With regard to the expansion of services, new e-mail systems will continue to appear both locally and internationally. Plans are already well advanced for a number of new e-mail systems around the world. Several of these will fall under the umbrella of the Association for Progressive Communications (APC).

In the course of this expansion it is likely that the APC will become a more diverse association. At present all APC host computers are similar and run similar software. For a variety of reasons, however, a number of the new additions will run on different types of system. The more heterogeneous nature of APC in the future will be offset by the fact that the network will expand to cover many new areas of the globe.

The facilities for non-commercial users on the GeoNet e-mail system, administered by Poptel, are also set to expand. Poptel has recently announced that it will be running a new GeoNet host computer in the city of Manchester in the north-west of England. This project is particularly significant since it is being organised and financed in conjunction with Manchester city council. The Manchester host will provide e-mail services to locally based groups, including community groups, local economic development agencies, small businesses, community enterprises and cooperatives.

Manchester is an industrial city and the local host will also be aiming to provide services to labour groups and workers' educational associations. A number of unions at the regional and national level have already expressed an interest in the project.

Besides providing facilities for the exchange of information, the Manchester host will also be a source of data on a wide range of topics. Among the databases that may be located on the host are: a local directory of women's businesses, a directory of Manchester resource centres, and information produced by the city council. Proposed trade union databases include a trade union directory and a health and safety database. It is also proposed to place a European-wide database of local environmental projects on the Manchester host.

In order to facilitate access to these new local resources, Manchester council and Poptel are investigating the possible creation of Electronic Village Halls or EVHs (another acronym!). These local centres would be provided with computer equipment so that they could be used for electronic communication or other computing tasks such as word processing, desk top publishing, or financial management.

The aim would be to encourage self-organisation and to provide experience in computer usage which could enhance people's employment prospects. The Electronic Village Hall proposal is strikingly similar to the 'community computing centres' which IBASE is hoping to establish in major cities in Brazil (see page 47). The idea of a 'techno bus' or mobile information technology centre is also under examination.

The Manchester project is interesting since it will cater for unions, commercial and non-commercial users. The emphasis is primarily local rather than non-commercial. This could foreshadow a broader trend towards the development of e-mail and bulletin board systems as sources of local community information.

The quality of service provided by e-mail systems should also continue to improve. As an example, e-mail systems may develop better capabilities for using graphic images as well as plain text. NGO e-mail networks can also be expected to play a leading role in the development of communications systems that use other scripts as well as the Latin script. Already NGOs in Thailand are using a small e-mail system/bulletin board that works in both English and Thai.

117

With regard to the second main trend — the integration of existing services — this will take two forms. Firstly, the interchange of messages between different technologies such as telex, fax and e-mail will continue to improve. The ability to receive fax into an e-mail box should move beyond the experimental stage and it should also become cheaper to send fax via e-mail.

Secondly, the links between different types of e-mail system will continue to improve. This tendency has been given a boost by the merger of Poptel/GeoNet and GreenNet at the administrative level (although they still run separate e-mail systems). This merger will certainly lead to the development of better links between the Poptel/GeoNet and GreenNet systems. By extension, there will also be better links between GeoNet and the other systems which fall under the umbrella of the Association for Progressive Communications (APC). Of equal significance, however, will be the development both of 'upward' links from the GeoNet/APC worlds to larger systems and 'downward' links to smaller systems.

The continuing development and spread of internationally agreed standards will make it far easier to transfer e-mail messages from GeoNet or APC systems to larger e-mail systems such as Dialcom/British Telecom Gold. It will not, however, necessarily become any cheaper since pricing will be determined primarily by the large operators.

More important will probably be the development of better gateways 'downwards' to the growing number of small e-mail systems. One such gateway that has recently been developed allows the exchange of messages between GeoNet/GreenNet and the Fido network. Fido is a software package that is commonly used on small, independent bulletin boards. It includes options to create automatic links with other Fido bulletin boards for the exchange of messages between users of different boards. In this manner an extensive network of independent Fido systems has evolved.

Fido systems are, relative to GeoNet or APC systems, cheap and easy to install. They do not require powerful computer hardware and do not use packet switching. For this reason they may be attractive in countries which do not have highly developed

118

computer and communication facilities or in situations where the number of users will be limited. The small NGO e-mail system in the Philippines, for example, uses Fido software. Fido, or a similar software package such as Major BBS, would be the likely choice for an e-mail system in most African countries.

The development of the Fidonet gateway illustrates the ongoing trend towards greater integration of the different types of e-mail system, offering different levels of service in a multi-layered, three dimensional model.

Increasingly the larger systems will offer comprehensive user directories, international communications, database services and an established public forum for the exchange of information between organisations, media workers, researchers and activists. The smaller systems, on the other hand, will offer a forum for more specialised topics or, alternatively, a platform for e-mail where other factors rule out the development of larger systems. The improved flow of information between the GeoNet/APC systems and the small systems will add a new dimension to the use of e-mail.

A further development may be the spread amongst e-mail users of off-line message handling. This is an adaption of techniques which are already established in the Fido world. The e-mail user runs software on the local microcomputer which allows for the preparation of e-mail messages or the reading of messages stored on the local computer at any time — without being connected to the e-mail system.

The software is installed so that it will automatically call the e-mail system at a predetermined time. It will then send to the e-mail system any new messages which are stored on the local microcomputer. New incoming messages stored in the mailbox on the e-mail host computer are copied to the local microcomputer where they will appear as 'new messages' the next time the user runs the local software on their microcomputer.

The microcomputer will typically call the e-mail host computer at a quiet time when call charges are cheap, for example, in the night. The transfer of messages might also use data compression techniques so that the call duration — and call charges — are kept to an absolute minimum.

119

The principle of off-line message handling is really no different from the normal procedures for uploading and downloading information but it is potentially more easy and cheaper to use. A software package for off-line message handling which is well-written and user friendly could go a long way towards improving the use of e-mail.

The past five years have witnessed the rapid growth of NGO e-mail systems and NGO networks. In many ways this book looks backwards — reflecting on these developments. But one thing is sure, the next five years will be just as exciting!

Glossary

APC see *Association for Progressive Communications*

ASCII American Standard Code for Information Interchange. A coding system that assigns letters of the alphabet, the numbers between 0 and 9, punctuation marks and computer 'control codes' to all the possible values of a byte. The seven-bit ASCII code covers the numbers 0000000 to 1111111 in binary, ie 0 to 127 in decimal. There is also an extended version of the ASCII code that defines the representation of all eight bits in a byte ie 0 to 255 in decimal. ASCII is used on all modern microcomputers. It is, in effect, a 'lowest common denominator' for information interchange. ASCII is widely used for swapping text messages on e-mail systems.

Association for Progressive Communications Umbrella organisation of seven non-profit e-mail systems. These are Alternex (Brazil), Fredsnaetet (Sweden), GreenNet (Britain), Nicarao (Nicaragua), PeaceNet/EcoNet/ConflictNet/HomeoNet (USA), Pegasus (Australia) and the Web (Canada).

Asynchronous (async) data transmission A form of data transmission in which the sending and receiving computers are not 'synchronised'. The transfer of each unit of data is preceded by a start bit indicating the beginning of transmission and is concluded by a stop bit indicating the end of transmission. This is also known as 'start/stop mode'. In synchronous communication, by contrast, the two modems are kept in constant synchronisation by the transmission of timing signals. Asynchronous transmission is always used in e-mail.

Baud Telecommunications term referring to the number of signalling elements per second carried by a communications

121

channel. Often used interchangeably with the term bits per second, although this is technically incorrect.

Bell standards Series of US modem standards developed by modem manufacturer Bell. Widespread in the Americas. Some Bell standards are not compatible with the CCITT equivalents that are used throughout Europe.

Binary file A non-text computer file. Word processing files, spreadsheet data files and computer programs are all examples of binary files.

Binary (representation/counting system) The binary counting system uses only 1s and 0s rather than the 10 digits used in our normal decimal counting system. The binary system is used to represent the two possible states — on or off — of electronic computer components.

Bit stands for 'binary digit'. A bit can only have two possible values: 1 or 0. The bit is the smallest unit of information used in a computer.

Bits per second (Bps) The normal measure of the speed of computer data transfer. Often used interchangeably with the term baud although this is technically incorrect.

Byte Group of eight bits representing one character such as a letter, number between 0 and 9, or a punctuation mark.

CCITT Comité Consultatif International Téléphonique et Télégraphique Committee of the International Telecommunications Union, which is in turn an agency of the United Nations. CCITT makes recommendations on standards for communications. The development of standards is of crucial importance to the development of telecommunications, and CCITT's recommendations are highly influential in this field.

Communications software package (comms software) A computer program which controls the transfer of data into and out of a computer. Communications software is always necessary for computer communications.

Data compression technique Coding techniques used to reduce the number of bits needed to transfer a given quantity of data. Data compression leads to an increased rate of data transfer. These techniques are most effective on text and graphics files.

Data Bit see *line settings*

Dedicated Refers to equipment which could be used for a number of tasks but is actually reserved solely for one task. For example, a fax machine might use a dedicated phone line.

Download Capture incoming data direct to disc.

Duplex (full/half) A full duplex communications channel can carry data in two directions simultaneously. A half duplex channel can carry data in two directions but only in one direction at a time. Full duplex communication is used in e-mail.

Error correction technique Method of ensuring (with a high degree of certainty) that data is transferred without corruption.

Expansion slots/cards All modern desk-top computers have some empty internal slots into which expansion cards can easily be fitted. These cards carry electronic circuitry to enhance the performance of the computer in various ways. They enable 'optional extras' to be used. Modems and serial ports are available on expansion cards.

File transfer protocol An agreed procedure for transmitting a computer file. A file transfer protocol must be used if non-text, binary files are being transferred. File transfer protocols such as X-modem and Kermit include provision for error correction, which helps to ensure that a file will be transferred error free.

Gateway A procedure for the regular transfer of messages between different e-mail systems.

GeoNet (GeoMail) Commercial e-mail system of West German origin consisting of a number of inter-linked GeoNet host computers. One of these hosts, based in London and run by Poptel, specialises in providing services for non-commercial users.

GreenNet E-mail system based in Britain. Member of APC network.

Handshaking An agreed system whereby either end of a communications link can cause a transmission to pause and resume. Software handshaking, used in e-mail, involves the transmission of pre-defined control codes to halt and re-start the flow of data.

Hayes compatibility Hayes is a large US modem manufacturer. The Hayes command language is a set of instructions used by a computer to control the operation of a modem. A modem is 'Hayes compatible' if it obeys the Hayes command set. The Hayes command set is a de facto standard in the modem industry.

Host computer The large central computer that actually 'runs' the e-mail system. Owned and operated by the body providing the e-mail service.

Interface A boundary across which data is passed from one piece of equipment to another. There is, for example, always a serial interface between a computer and a modem.

Kermit Together with X-modem, the most common file transfer protocol encountered on e-mail systems.

Line setting Refers collectively to the setting of a number of variables that influence the process of data transfer. These include the settings for data bits, start bits, stop bits, parity and speed. Both computers must operate with the same line settings.

Log off The procedure for disconnecting from an e-mail host computer.

Log in/log on The procedure for connecting up with an e-mail host computer. This may involve typing in various identification codes and passwords.

Mirror A communications software package.

MNP Microcom Networking Protocol. Error correction and data compression techniques developed by modem manufacturers Microcom. There are several 'layers' or 'classes'. MNP up to level 5 will be encountered on some packet switching or e-mail systems.

Modem Stands for 'modulator demodulator'. A modem converts digital data from a computer into an analogue form which can be transmitted over a telephone line, and vice versa. At present, a modem is always needed for computer communication over the telephone system.

Network User Address (NUA) The unique address of a packet terminal on a packet switching system. E-mail users will need to know the NUA of their e-mail host computer if they plan to access the system via packet switching.

Network User Identity (NUI) Unique identity code allocated to every user of a packet switching system. Acts as a password into the system and as a control for billing purposes.

Non-Governmental Organisation (NGO) Any organisation working on social, development or international issues that is independent of direct state control. Typically used to describe large development agencies.

NUA see *Network User Address*

NUI see *Network User Identity*

Packet Assembler Disassembler (PAD) A device that converts asynchronous data from an ordinary microcomputer into 'packets' for transfer across a packet switching network, and vice versa. E-mail host computers are fitted with their own PAD. Ordinary

125

e-mail subscribers use public PADs situated in their local Packet Switching Exchange (PSE).

Packet switching (systems/networks) A technique for cheap and efficient computer data transmission. A stream of computer data is broken down into discrete packets that are sent separately across the packet switching network before being reassembled and forwarded to the destination. A packet switching network consists of a matrix of computers capable of sending and receiving packets of data.

Public packet switching systems are available in many countries. All these public national systems are linked together in an international packet switching system. The technical details of packet switching are defined in a recommendation of the CCITT known as 'X25'. Packet switching systems may also be referred to as X25 networks.

Packet Switching Exchange (PSE) An exchange on a public packet switching network. The PSE will house a Packet Assembler Disassembler. The PSE is the point of entry into the packet switching network for ordinary microcomputer users.

Packet terminal A computer capable of sending and receiving packets of data across a packet switching system. Ordinary microcomputers are not packet terminals.

PAD see *Packet Assembler Disassembler*

Parallel (interface/data transfer) Data transmission of one byte (ie eight bits) at a time as opposed to serial transmission which involves the sending of one bit at a time. A printer is usually linked to a computer through a parallel interface.

Parity bit see *line settings*

PDN see *Public Data Network*

PeaceNet E-mail system based in the USA. Administered by the Institute for Global Communications. Member of APC network.

126

Port A 'socket' through which data is passed. A computer, for example, must have a serial port if it is to be connected by a cable to an external modem.

Procomm A popular communications software package. Available as 'shareware' at a price that is far lower then commercial rates.

PSE see *Packet Switching Exchange*

PSS (Packet SwitchStream) The public packet switching system of British Telecom in Britain. Currently being supplemented by the more modern Dialplus system.

Public Data Network (PDN) A public packet switching system.

RS-232 The most common type of serial interface found on microcomputers. RS-232 is an American standard. V24 is the equivalent CCITT recommendation.

Serial (interface/data transfer) Data transmission one bit at a time as opposed to parallel transmission which involves transmission of one byte (ie eight bits) at a time. A modem is always linked to a computer through a serial interface.

Standards Standards are vitally important in the field of telecommunications. Standards have been defined for modems, fax, computer data interchange, packet switching and so forth. Without these standards, communication between different countries or between the equipment of different manufacturers would be a nightmare.

Start bit see *line settings*

Stop bit see *line settings*

Text file A file consisting entirely of ASCII text characters. Does not contain any of the special ASCII control codes except for carriage return and the end of file code. The opposite of a binary file which may contain non-text information or control codes. Most e-mail users swap messages as plain ASCII text transmissions.

Upload Send a file direct from disc.

V24 See *RS-232*

V42 CCITT recommendation for an error correction technique for modems.

V-series recommendations Set of CCITT standards relating to computer data transfer over telephone networks. All the recommendations begin with a V, eg V22, V23. Includes recommendations for modems.

X-modem Together with Kermit, the most common file transfer protocol encountered on e-mail systems.

Appendix A

Step by step guide to getting on-line

This section aims to provide a simple step by step guide to getting on-line for people who are new to e-mail. It is intended for any kind of user, anywhere in the world, using any e-mail system... so it is necessarily quite general. It is basically a set of guidelines that cover the important points in a logical order. You — the reader — will have to do all the research for your particular e-mail system yourself.

1. *Choose your e-mail system*

   Which e-mail system will you use? Contact organisations similar to your own to learn of their experiences. Contact your partners, the organisations with which you wish to communicate. Do they use e-mail? If not, check which systems they might be able to use. Contact major organisations using e-mail (such as those listed in Appendix B) to seek their advice. Above all, contact the e-mail systems themselves. They are the experts and they are happy to help.

   Major considerations in choosing a system will be:
   - Is it practical to connect up to the system from your geographical location?
   - Who else uses the system?
   - Do your partners use the same system, or can they potentially do so?
   - What are the e-mail system charges?
   - What are the costs of connecting up to the system from your geographical location?
   - What gateways are available to other e-mail systems that your partners might be using?

2. *Training, training, training!*

Budget time and money for appropriate staff training now. The e-mail system will be able to give advice on where to go for training or alternatively put you in contact with other experienced users. In a large organisation a number of staff will eventually need to acquire e-mail skills. It is no good getting into a situation where you rely entirely on one expert. Make sure that key staff have plenty of opportunity to familiarise themselves with the system.

If you can't make a commitment to comprehensive training then you should seriously reconsider the idea of adopting e-mail.

3. *Choose how to connect up with your preferred e-mail system*

Through packet switching or by direct dial? Assuming that packet switching is a viable option from your geographical location, then this question will be decided primarily by cost considerations. On long distance calls, access via packet switching will normally be cheaper. On shorter calls the decision will involve a complicated calculation involving a number of factors. In many cases, direct dial may be a possibility if you can afford the initial investment for a high-speed, error-correcting modem. The e-mail system will be able to offer advice.

4. *Contact your local packet switching system*

Check the prices for joining and for usage. Check the procedure for obtaining a Network User Identity (which you need before you can use the system). In some countries obtaining an NUI and getting the local packet switching system to work on international calls are the two slowest and most bureaucratic stages. So start early and leave plenty of time.

5. *Choose a modem*

Your choice of modem will be based on the requirements of the e-mail system and, if you are using it, your local packet switching system. Important considerations include:

- Compatibility with your existing computer and telephone system
- Bell or CCITT standards?
- Speed
- Built-in error-correction, such as MNP?
- Internal or external?

Under normal circumstances, make sure that the modem you choose is Hayes compatible. If you plan to get an external modem, then remember to check whether your computer will need to have a serial port fitted. Don't forget the cost of the modem cable.

6. *Double checking*

Before you purchase the modem, check with the e-mail system and the packet switching company that it is suitable. For an inexperienced user it is generally a false economy to buy the cheapest possible modem by mail order or from an unreliable source. It is far better to pay a little more to a reputable dealer who can help with advice and installation.

If you are planning to use a telephone line running through a switchboard, you had better double-check with the dealer that the modem will work. Alternatively, ask to see the modem working through the switchboard before you pay any money. Otherwise you might find that you also need a separate external phone line for e-mail.

7. *Choose a communications software package*

This will largely be a matter of taste and money. Assuming that you will be using a Hayes compatible modem, then the only thing to watch out for is that the software package provides all the file transfer protocols offered by your chosen e-mail system. X-modem and Kermit are the absolute minimum. In addition, you might consider spending a little more to buy a software package that offers MNP error correction. Other things being equal, Procomm or Procomm Plus are basic, cheap packages that are perfectly adequate for normal e-mail usage.

Remember to make a backup of the master disc before you use the software!

8. *Install and test the modem and the software*
This includes physically attaching the modem to the computer and setting up the software so that it will do what you want. An inexperienced user may need some help at this point. The manual for the modem will probably contain some simple test routines to check whether everything is working. A common initial problem is that the modem is attached to a serial port called 'COM1', while the software is installed to talk to a second serial port called 'COM2', or vice versa. If this is the case, nothing at all will happen when commands are issued from the computer.

Trial and error, patience and a pioneering spirit are all required at this stage. Take some time to learn the basic commands you will need in order to use the communications software. These include the commands to dial a number, to upload a file, to download a file, and to disconnect a call.

9. *Connect up to the e-mail system*
In the case of access via a packet switching system, you will need:

- The line settings required by your local packet switching system. These are the settings for data bits, parity, stop bits and transmission speed. Your software should normally be set to distant echo (also know as 'full duplex').
- The telephone number of your local Packet Switching Exchange. On some systems there will be different telephone numbers for different transmission speeds.
- Your Network User Identity.
- The Network User Address of the e-mail system. You can get this from the e-mail system.
- Instructions explaining how to place a call on your local packet switching system. These will be available from the local packet switching company.

If you dial direct to the e-mail system, you will need:

- The line settings required by the e-mail system (as described above).

● The direct dial telephone number of the e-mail system.

In both cases you will need to know the basic commands to use once you are actually connected to the e-mail system. These include logging on (ie giving your name and password), reading mail, sending mail, logging off.

10. *Trouble-shooting*
Things probably won't go right the first time! It is often difficult to determine exactly where problems are occurring. It could be in the communications software, the modem, the packet switching system or the e-mail system. It is normally easiest to consult direct with the e-mail system, in which case be sure that you have made clear notes of exactly what you did and what happened. The more detail you can provide, the easier it is to track down the problem.

Here are a few common problems and possible solutions:

● **You place a call by packet switching but can't manage to get right through to the e-mail system.**
  If you are making an international call, you may well experience initial problems in getting the call routed across the international connections. It may be that you are not giving the NUA (Network User Address) in exactly the right form. Check that you don't need an extra prefix or suffix.

● **The modem dials through to the packet switching exchange or e-mail system but then the call is dropped.**
  It could be that the Packet Switching Exchange or e-mail system is engaged or not working. Try again later, preferably at a less busy time of day. Alternatively, it could be that the line settings in your software are not set up correctly — they may not correspond to what is expected by the Packet Switching Exchange or e-mail system. This is one of the most common initial problems. Double check the settings. Try altering them and see if this has any effect.

133

- **A connection is established but the screen fills up with strings of strange characters instead of proper words.**

  This is almost certainly because your data bit, parity bit or stop bit setting is wrong.

- **A connection is established and you succeed in communicating with the e-mail system but suddenly strings of strange characters appear on the screen. The connection may also be lost.**

  This could be due to line noise. Using a file transfer protocol or error correction can alleviate the effects. Line noise may be the result of a number of factors. It is worth checking to see if it is better at a different time of day.

  Keep an open mind and experiment to see if anything helps. My own organisation suffered severe problems due to line noise even on local data calls. Then one day the interference stopped and has never been a problem since. I still don't know why.

- **You are sending a long message. Everything is going fine, but then suddenly you lose the connection.**

  Some systems will cut out or cause other problems if you try to send very long messages. Try splitting the message up and re-sending in smaller sections.

11. *Learning about the e-mail system*

The first few times you go into a system it may be an idea to 'log' your entire call. This means that you capture everything that happens to disc. You can then print out the log of the session and use it as notes the next time you use the system. All communications packages will have some kind of log or capture facility.

Of course, once you have actually managed to get in to the e-mail system a couple of times then you will always be able to get plenty of help. If you have any problems, then post a message on an appropriate bulletin board or conference. You will normally receive plenty of replies from dedicated e-mail users eager to share their knowledge with a new recruit.

Finally

If you have backups of all your software then you can't do any permanent damage whilst using e-mail. So remember: DON'T PANIC. If you get really stuck then just unplug the modem and, if necessary, switch off the computer. In the beginning you will need to experiment with the system. This may cause you to waste some time and money. In the long run, however, this will prove well spent if it helps you to become a more efficient e-mail user.

There is a saying that runs: 'If all else fails, read the instructions!'. Unfortunately for e-mail users, it is imperative that you read the instructions BEFORE you start. The e-mail system will provide a manual, the packet switching system will provide instructions for use, there will be a manual with the communications software and one with the modem. A glance at the basic information contained in these guides is invaluable if you want to save time and avoid frustration.

Good luck !!!

Appendix B

Contact list of e-mail systems and consultants

It is impractical to give addresses for all the organisations listed below. The contact details, particularly of the smaller systems, may be subject to alteration. The addresses of a number of the larger systems, however, are given in Appendix C. It should be easy to get more details on the smaller systems from these larger organisations.

Alternex E-mail system based in Brazil. Member of APC network. About 250 users. See IBASE.

AMRC Asia Monitor Resource Centre. Labour and union research department based in Hong Kong. Much experience in the use of electronic communications by NGOs in Asia.

Antenna Technical advisory group working for various NGO networks and international organisations. Its main focus is on documentation and communication. Antenna acts as facilitator for the Interdoc network.

CCAN Computer Communication Access for NGOs. NGO bulletin board system based in Thailand. Five active users.

ConflictNet E-mail network based in the USA. Administered by IGC.

Chasque NGO e-mail system based in Uruguay. 17 NGO users and about 200 individuals (many on a trial basis).

CRIES	NGO research organisation based in Nicaragua. Runs the Nicarao e-mail system.
DESCO	NGO with much experience in the use of e-mail. Located in Peru.
EcoNet	E-mail network based in the USA. Administered by IGC.
EDRC	Environment and Development Resource Centre based in Belgium. International association promoting sustainable development through projects such as a database on environment and development NGOs and resource material on environmental and developmental issues and events.
EIES	E-mail system based in USA. Some NGO users.
ELCI	Environment Liaison Centre International, Kenya. Proposing to start a small e-mail system based in Nairobi.
FORO	Colombian regional network
Fredsnaetet	E-mail system based in Sweden. Member of APC network. About 200 users. Also known as PeaceNet Sweden.
GeoNet	Commercial e-mail system run on host computers in Europe and the USA. The British-based GEO2 host is run by Poptel and specialises in providing services to the non-commercial sector. About 600 users.
Global Dialog	Organisation working to improve information exchange between USSR, USA, Western Europe and Japan.
GreenNet	E-mail system based in Britain. Member of APC network. About 850 users.

137

HomeoNet   Homeopathy network based on APC e-mail systems such as IGC and GreenNet.

Huridocs   International human rights network.

IBASE   Research NGO based in Brazil. Experienced computer users. Runs Alternex e-mail system.

IGC   Institute for Global Communications. Non-commercial organisation which administers the ConflictNet, EcoNet, HomeoNet and PeaceNet e-mail systems in the USA. There are about 4,500 users belonging to IGC networks.

ILET   NGO with much experience of electronic communications. Located in Chile.

Interdoc   International information technology and e-mail network.

Mango BBS   NGO bulletin board/e-mail system based in Zimbabwe. About five users.

MCI   Major commercial e-mail system based in the USA.

Nicarao   E-mail system based in Nicaragua. Member of the APC network. About 120 users.

PeaceNet   E-mail network based in the USA. Administered by IGC.

Pegasus   E-mail system based in Australia. Member of the APC network. About 600 users.

People's Access BBS   E-mail system/NGO bulletin board based in the Philippines. Used by about 35 organisations and 200 individuals.

Poptel   London based organisation which specialises in providing services for non-commercial users on the GeoNet e-mail system. Part of the Soft Solution cooperative.

Satis   International network of organisations working for sustainable development.

Soft Solution   London based cooperative that administers the Poptel/GeoNet and GreenNet e-mail systems.

TCN   The Telecommunications Cooperative Network. E-mail system based in the USA.

Web   E-mail system based in Canada. Member of the APC network. About 500 users.

WorkNet   Progressive e-mail system based in South Africa. Almost 100 users, including the alternative press, trade unions, church and other progressive groups.

Appendix C

Contact addresses

Conventions
Telephone numbers are given in their full international form, including country code. A '+' before a telephone number means 'establish an international call'. The procedure for doing this varies from country to country. In Britain, for example, a number is preceded by '010' for an international call. Readers in Britain dialling a British number should replace the '+44' with '0'.

Mailbox names on APC e-mail systems (Alternex, GreenNet, Nicarao, PeaceNet Sweden, PeaceNet USA, Pegasus and the Web) must be used in lower case.

Alternex
Same as IBASE

AMRC
Address: 444 Nathan Road, 8-B, Kowloon, Hong Kong
Tel: +852-3321-346
E-mail: GeoNet GEO2: AMRC, Pegasus amrc

Antenna
Address: PO Box 1513, 6501 BM Nijmegen, Netherlands
Tel: +31-80-235372
E-mail: GeoNet GEO2:ANTENNA-NL, GreenNet antennanl, Alternex antenna

Chasque
Address: Miguel del Corro 1461, Montevideo 11200, Uruguay
Tel: +598-2496192
E-mail: GeoNet GEO2:CHASQUE, PeaceNet chasque

CIIR
Address: 22 Coleman Fields, London N1 7AF, UK
Tel: +44-71-354-0883
E-mail: GeoNet GEO2:CIIR, GreenNet ciirlon

EDRC
Address: Blvd Louis Schmidtlaan 26, 1040 Brussels, Belgium
Tel: +32-2-7368050
E-mail: GeoNet GEO2:EDRC

ELCI
Address: Box 72461, Nairobi, Kenya
Tel: +254-2-562015
E-mail: GreenNet elcidwr

Friends of the Earth
Address: FoE UK and FoE International Secretariat, 26-28 Underwood Street, London N1 7JQ, UK
Tel: +44-71-490-1555
E-mail: GreenNet foe

Global Dialog Association
Address: TeleXphone SARL, BP 517, F-13813 Vitrolles cedex, France
Tel: +33-90758927
E-mail: GeoNet TLXF:GLOBAL-MAIL

Huridocs
Address: Torggate 27, N-0183 Oslo 1, Norway
Tel: +47-2-200247
E-mail: GeoNet GEO2:HURIDOCS

IBASE
Address: Rua Vicente de Souza 29, Botafogo, 22251 Rio de Janeiro RJ, Brazil
Tel: +55-21-286-0348
E-mail: GeoNet GEO2:IBASE, PeaceNet ibase, Alternex ibase.

141

Institute for Global Communications (for ConflictNet, EcoNet and PeaceNet)
Address:	3228 Sacramento Street, San Francisco CA 94115, USA
Tel:	+1-415-9230900
E-mail:	On all APC systems messages can be addressed to IGC:support

Interdoc facilitator
Address:	Michael Polman, c/o Antenna (see separate entry)

**Interdoc chair of international steering group 1990/91
Interdoc Asia**

Interdoc Africa
Address:	Dianah Macharia, c/o ELCI (see separate entry)

Interdoc Asia
Address:	Roberto Verzola, c/o People's Access (see separate entry

Interdoc Europe
Address:	Graham Lane, c/o CIIR (see separate entry)

Interdoc Latin America
Address:	Anabel Cruz, c/o IOCU-LAC, Casilla 10993, Sucursal 2, Montevideo, Uruguay
Tel:	+598-2-920216
E-mail:	Geonet GE02:IOCU-LAC, Alternex iocu

Interdoc North America
Address:	Tom Fenton, c/o Third World Resources, 464 19 Street, Oakland, CA 94612 - 9761, USA
Tel:	+1-415-8354692
E-mail	PeaceNet tfenton

Mango
Address:	MANGO/SAPES trust, 4 Rowland Square, Milton Park, Harare, Zimbabwe
Tel:	+263-4-723518
E-mail:	C/O GeoNet GEO2:AIA, GreenNet aiazim

142

Nicarao
Address: CRIES, Apartado postal C-163, Managua,
            Nicaragua
Tel: +505-2-25137
E-mail: PeaceNet cries, Nicarao cries

Pegasus
Address: PO Box 424, Byron Bay, NSW 2481, Australia
Tel: +61-66-856789
E-mail: Pegasus pegasus

People's Access
Address: PO Box 9121, MCS Mailing Center, Pasong
            Tamo, Makati, Metro Manila, Philippines
Tel: +63-2-971535 (used for ACCESS bulletin board
            outside office hours)
E-mail: GeoNet GEO2:ACCESS, PeaceNet paces

Satis
Address: PO Box 17227, 1001 GE Amsterdam, The
            Netherlands
Tel: +31-20-260619
E-mail: GeoNet GEO2:SATIS

Soft Solution (for GreenNet and Poptel/GeoNet)
Address: 25 Downham Road, London N1 5AA, UK
Tel: +44-71-249-2948 or +44-71-923-2624
E-mail: GeoNet GEO2:POPTEL-ADMIN, GreenNet
            support

Web
Address: NIRV Centre, 456 Spandina Ave, 2nd fl, Toronto
            M5T 2G8, Canada
Tel: +1-416-9290634
E-mail: Web spider

Worknet
Address: PO Box 157, Johannesburg 2000, South Africa
Tel: +27-11-230437
E-mail: GeoNet GEO2:WORKNET, GreenNet worknet

Reading list

There is not much material available about e-mail that is relevant to the non-commercial sector. Consequently this is rather a poor list. Many of the titles mentioned are quite technical and only partially relevant to someone interested in e-mail.

Telephone numbers are given in their full international form, including country code. '+' before a telephone number means 'establish an international call'. The procedure for doing this varies from country to country. In Britain, for example, a number is preceded by '010' for an international call. Readers in Britain dialling a British number should replace the '+44' with '0'.

Title: **BACT: A basic guide to telex, electronic mail and fax services for small businesses**
Type: Booklet (21 pages)
Address: Oftel Library,
Atlantic House,
Holborn Viaduct
London EC1N 2HQ, UK
Tel +44-71-822-1688
Details: Free
Description: Very simple slim booklet. Suitable for someone completely new to the field of telecommunications.

Title: **The CASE pocket book of computer communications**
Type: Pocket book (92 pages)
Address: CASE Communications,
PO Box 254,
Caxton Way,
Watford Business Park,
Watford,
Herts WD1 8XH, UK
Tel +44-923-58000
Details: Free
Description: For advanced comms users. Very technical but useful summary of telecommunications jargon and concepts. Philips produce a similar pocket book.

Title:	**Communicate**
Type:	Monthly magazine
Address:	'Communicate',
	Link House,
	Dingwall Avenue,
	Croydon CR9 2TA, UK
	Tel +44-81-686-2599
Details:	Free for qualified telecommunications 'professionals'.
Description:	Telecommunications magazine aimed at professionals and the corporate market. Regularly carries small items of interest to e-mailers, occasionally major features.

Title:	**Communicating with microcomputers** by Ian Cullimore
Type:	Book (209 pages)
Address:	(Publisher)
	Sigma Press
	98a Water Lane
	Wilmslow
	Cheshire SK9 5BB, UK
Details:	ISBN 1-85058-055-3
Description:	Very readable technical book covering general aspects of microcomputer communications such as serial and parallel interfaces, communications packages, file transfer protocols, Kermit etc

Title:	**Communications International**
Type:	Monthly magazine
Address:	Communications International,
	100 Avenue Road,
	London NW3 3TP, UK
	Tel +44-71-935-6611
Details:	Free to suitably qualified business users in the field of electronic communications.
Description:	Carries telecommunications business news rather than reviews of the latest modems. Good source of international news.

Title:	**Contact-0**
Type:	Newsletter of Interdoc network
Address:	Contact Antenna or People's Access (details in appendix C)

145

Description: The main international e-mail newsletter. The Spanish edition appears regularly, the English edition has appeared erratically.

Title: **Electronic communications - International Labour Reports** by Alison Ali
Type: Article (5 pages) in *Women in Computing Newsletter*
Address: Women and Computing,
c/o Mycrosyster,
Wild Court,
off Kingsway,
London WC2B 5AU, UK
Tel +44-71-430-0655
Details: *Women and Computing Newsletter* No. 28, April 1989
Description: Examines how the magazine International Labour Report uses e-mail to exchange information with labour-orientated organisations around the world, to commission and save articles direct to disc, and to assist workers' and human rights campaigns. Questions why there are so few women and women's organisations using e-mail.

Title: **Electronic mail: communication for beginners**
Type: Book (46 pages)
Address: TWIN,
345 Goswell Road,
London EC1V 7JT, UK
Tel +44-71-837-8222
e-mail: GEO2:TWIN
Details: ISBN: 0-948525-04-5
Description: Simple introduction to e-mail based on the experiences of TWIN Trading. Attractively produced with nice cartoons.

Title: **Email - Africa's Window on the World** by Celia Mather
Type: Article (2 pages)in *Computers in Africa*
Address: Computers in Africa,
Africa File Ltd,
21 Mill Lane,
London NW6 1NT, UK
Tel +44-71-794-5308
e-mail GEO2:AFRICA-FILE

Details: *Computers in Africa* Vol.4 No.4, June 1990
Description Report on the progress made in setting up e-mail systems by and for progressive organisations in Africa.

Title: **First Steps in Packet Switching**
Type: Booklet (64 pages)
Address: British Telecom,
81 Newgate Street,
London EC1A 7AJ, UK
Tel +44-71-356-5000
Details: Free. BT book reference PH/NN 173(3/86)
Description: Excellent introduction for anyone who wants to get into the technical side of packet switching. Don't be misled by the title — this publication contains plenty of technical detail.

Title: **Hacker's Handbook III** by Hugo Cornwall
Type: Book (230 pages)
Address: Century Hutchinson Ltd,
62-65 Chandos Place,
London WC2N 4NW, UK
Details: ISBN 0-7126-1147-9. Published 1988.
Description: Entertaining book giving inside information on some famous 'hacks'. Also a very useful handbook for anyone interested in straightforward data communications. Thoroughly recommended. *Note: due to the new Computer Misuse law this book was withdrawn in the UK as of September 1990.*

Title: **International Data Services: A Guide for Business Personal Computer Users**
Type: Booklet (80 pages)
Address: British Telecom International,
Holborn Centre,
120 Holborn,
London EC1N 2TE, UK
Tel +44-71-492-2000
Details: Free
Description: Excellent introduction to data communications and packet switching. Useful emphasis on the international aspects of data communications. It is written for British

147

readers but could also be helpful to users in other countries. Recommended.

Title: **Labour goes On-Line** by David Spooner
Type: Article (2 pages) in International Labour Reports
Address: International Labour Reports,
               PO Box 45,
               Stainborough,
               Barnsley S75 3EA, UK
               Tel +44-226-730023
               e-mail GEO2:ILR
Details: International Labour Reports, issue 27-28, Summer 1988
Description: Looks at the responses by trade unions around the world to new communication technology.

Title: **Media Development** (including Communication Resource)
Type: Quarterly magazine
Address: World Association for Christian Communication,
               357 Kennington Lane,
               London SE11 5QY, UK
               Tel +44-71-582-9139
Description: Interesting magazine and supplement looking at general issues of communication from a non-commercial perspective.

Title: **The Network**
Type: Magazine (4 issues per year)
Address: TWIN,
               345 Goswell Road,
               London EC1V 7JT, UK
               Tel +44-71-837-8222
               e-mail GEO2:TWIN
Details: Free to Third World networkers
Description: Useful magazine covering all aspects of 'networking'. Sometimes has articles on e-mail.

Title: **Online — Interdoc 1984-1990**
Type: Booklet
Address: IDOC Resource Centre,
               Via Santa Maria dell'Anima 30,
               00186 Rome,

Italy
Tel: +39-6-6868332
e-mail: GeoNet GEO2:IDOC

Details: 36 page booklet. Price $5.00

Description: Useful compilation of articles relating to and arising from the work of Interdoc. Prepared for the large Interdoc meeting held in the Netherlands in May 1990.

Title: **PC:User**

Type: Fortnightly magazine

Address: (circulation inquiries)
PC:User magazine,
Priory Court,
30-32 Farringdon Lane,
London EC1R 3AU, UK

Details: Free to 'selected senior managers'

Description: Just one out of a plethora of PC magazines aimed at the corporate sector. Regularly carries useful reviews on new modems, communications software, fax cards and other related comms material.

Title: **The Philips Pocket Book of Telecommunications**

Type: Pocket book (149 pages)

Address: Philips Business Systems,
Elektra House,
Bergholt Road,
Colchester,
Essex CO4 5BE, UK
Tel +44-206-575115

Details: Free

Description: Pocket booklet covering telecommunications jargon and general principles. Similar to a pocket booklet produced by CASE.

Title: **Trade Unions On-Line: The International Labour Movement and Computer Communications** by Celia Mather and Ben Lowe

Type: Report and directory (60 pages)

Address: International Labour Reports,
PO Box 45,
Stainborough,

149

                    Barnsley S75 3EA, UK

                    Tel +44-226-730023

                    e-mail: GEO2:ILR

Details: Published by Independent Labour Reports, September 1990

Description: Report on the growing use of e-mail by trade unions and workers' organisations worldwide; includes case studies of international, British and Scandinavian union organisations, and also discussions on labour-produced databases. Plus a directory of labour movement e-mail users worldwide.

Title: **What to Buy for Business**

Type: Magazine (10 issues per year)

Address: What to Buy plc,
11 Kings Road,
London SW3 4RP, UK
Tel +44-71-730-0403

Description: Magazine covering standard office equipment. Each issue concentrates on a different topic and reviews all available makes. Periodically does excellent reports on the fax market. Has also done issues on telex, microcomputers, printers etc.

Title: **Women On-Line** by Frances Ellery

Type: Article (2 pages) in *Women and Computing Newsletter*

Address: Women and Computing,
c/o Mycrosyster,
Wild Court, off Kingsway,
London WC2B 5AU, UK
Tel: +44-71-430-0655

Details: *Women and Computing No. 31*, mid-1990

Description: Report on women's discussions and action at the Interdoc conference Information Exchange for Social Change in the Netherlands, May 1990. Highlights the facts that, with few women using e-mail, information through computers is still predominantly controlled by men

150

Index

Numbers in italics refer to diagrams.

151

Antenna, PO Box 1513, 6501 BM Nijmegen, The Netherlands
Tel: +31-80-235372
E-mail: GeoNet GEO2:ANTENNA-NL, GreenNet antennanl, Alternex antenna

Antenna is a technical advisory group working for a variety of NGO networks and international organisations. Its main focus is documentation and communication. It organises seminars, conferences and workshops around the world. As facilitator and contact point for Interdoc, Antenna helps members to appropriate and implement new technologies. It also organises NGO database host systems and compiles directories of NGOs using electronic mail, telex and telefax.

Antenna seeks to coordinate training and support for NGOs in computer communications and documentation. Information from individuals or organisations needing or offering help in these fields is welcome.

E-mail users with advanced technical inquiries and problems relating to computer communications are invited to contact Antenna.

CIIR

CIIR, 22 Coleman Fields, London N1 7AF, UK
Tel: +44-71-354 0883
E-mail: GEO2:CIIR, GreenNet, ciirlon

The Catholic Institute for International Relations (CIIR), founded in 1940, works to promote justice and development in the Third World.

Our Overseas Programme sends experienced professionals to share their skills in small-scale community development projects in Latin America, Africa and the Middle East. CIIR works with people of any religious belief or none.

Our Education and Publishing Programme provides information on socio-economic, political, church and human rights issues in developing countries. Its work focusses on the structures of injustice that prevent development for the Third World's poor.

CIIR members receive CIIR News five times a year and a copy of each new issue of *Comment* to keep you up-to-date with development issues, and you get special discounts on other CIIR publications. The annual membership subscription is £5 (unwaged), £15 (UK) or £20 (overseas).

Environment & Development Resource Centre (EDRC), Blvd Louis
Schmidtlaan 26, 1040 Brussels, Belgium
Tel: +32-2-7368050
E-mail: GeoNet GEO2:EDRC

EDRC is an international non-profit association established in 1988. It
works to promote global sustainable development worldwide that is
ecologically sound, socially just and respectful of cultural diversity.

EDRC carries out research and development, monitoring and
publishing in the field of the environment and development, often with
an emphasis on international environmental economics and law. It has
undertaken and promoted research, for example, on the environmental
impact of international trade. EDRC also assists in the organisation of
international conferences and working groups.

Interdoc, c/o Antenna, PO Box 1513, 6501 BM Nijmegen, The
Netherlands
E-mail: GeoNet GEO2:INTERDOC, PeaceNet interdoc

Interdoc is an international and interdisciplinary partnership of NGOs
and NGO networks using information for social change. It is structured
around the international on-line network and has members on most NGO
mailbox host systems. Interdoc comprises the world's largest user-group
of NGOs that use electronic mail for networking.

Interdoc has a regionalised structure (see Appendix C for contact
addresses) with an international chair that rotates on a yearly basis.
Antenna acts as Interdoc's facilitator and as contact point for the network.